T0194153

POWER
TO LIVE

Harnessing the Power That God
Gives Us to Live Today

BILL ADKINS

WESTBOW
PRESS®
A DIVISION OF THOMAS NELSON
& ZONDERVAN

Scripture taken from the King James Version of the Bible

Scripture quotations marked NIV are taken from the Holy Bible, New International Version. NIV. Copyright 1973, 1978, 1984 by International Bible Society. Used by permission of Zondervan. All rights reserved.

Scripture quotations marked NASB are taken from the New American Standard Bible, Copyright 1960, 1962, 1963, 1968, 1971, 1972, 1973, 1975, 1977, 1995 byThe Lockman Foundation. Used by permission.

Scripture quotations marked NLT are taken from the Holy Bible, New Living Translation, copyright 1996, 2004, 2007. Used by permission of Tyndale House Publishers, Inc. Carol Stream, Illinois 60188. All rights reserved.

WestBow Press books may be ordered through booksellers or by contacting:

WestBow Press
A Division of Thomas Nelson & Zondervan
1663 Liberty Drive
Bloomington, IN 47403
www.westbowpress.com
1 (866) 928-1240

ISBN: 978-1-5127-8812-9 (sc)
ISBN: 978-1-5127-8813-6 (hc)
ISBN: 978-1-5127-8811-2 (e)

Library of Congress Control Number: 2017908064

Print information available on the last page.

WestBow Press rev. date: 4/1/2017

PROLOGUE

For all of my life I have been a Christian and a member of a church body. There were brief periods when I was a member of more than a single church and denomination. Educated Catholic, mentored by Disciples of Christ and preached to by Baptists, I thought I had enough religious preparation for my coming years. But with all of the above I found myself wanting and desperately seeking some direction for my living. You see it was my living that needed assistance. All of my prior religious experience prepared me for dying and death. Heaven being my focus and goal left me without substantial information on what to do on this earth before I arrived in the Kingdom.

Now what happened to me is exactly what I don't want to happen to everyone else. I stumbled, backslid a couple hundred times, made mistake after mistake, bad choice after bad choice, had disaster after disaster, calamity after calamity, good fortune, bad fortune, then good fortune and bad fortune again. I literally spent the first forty-two years of my life confused and disoriented. There were some successes and achievements however my spiritual ability was null and void. What I accomplished, I accomplished, and what I accomplished, I could not sustain. My life was the proverbial roller coaster with countless numbers of "ups and downs." What I longed for was some kind of spiritual stability that would influence my life, my living. I had the seed of God's Word planted in me, but it was ineffectual because I did not know how to activate it.

Here is the problem; the manner by which I received God's Word did not take firm root. I heard it but I did not truly receive it. How many sermons have I heard? Thousands. How many sermons did I need to hear; one which would take root in me. I needed one good message teaching me how to live and how to apply God's Holy Word to my daily living. All of us need to know how to manifest our faith into daily action. As I look back I realize that most of the sermons I heard did not have enough "how to" information to manifest them into my living. Nothing profoundly touched me. It is not my point to simply decry my pastors of the past. They were all good men, serving God to the absolute best of their ability. It was, and still is to some degree, the culture of the church that left the void. Some people come to church looking for God and the church gets in the way. It is the culture of some churches that prove counterproductive to successful living. My Catholicism was wrapped in mysticism and I never bought into that. As a Disciple of Christ member I was bored and as a Baptist I was bewildered.

Faith does come by hearing, but what type of hearing? I suggest that we need to be taught how to hear. I listened, but I did not hear. I remember the story of Ray Charles, the singer, blind from his early childhood being confronted by a policeman when caught driving a car with the assistance of an employee. The policeman asked the singer, "Why do you think you can drive a car Mr. Charles?" Charles replied, "I'm just blind, that does not mean that I can't see!" Ray Charles understood that he could see through the eyes of others, however blind himself. There are times when our vision is impaired and we need guidance. There must be willingness and a longing when we hear God's Word. There must be a "seeking-after" attitude that creates the pathway from the ear to the heart. Pastors and preachers must know that homiletical perfection and hermeneutical excellence will not always accomplish the task of delivering a good sermon. The power in preaching is in what comes from the heart to reach another heart. I will dare to say that the power of one good testimony will out perform most sermons. But we preach, and continue to preach, for the purpose of faith. It is the duty of the listener, the worship attendee, to seek after the manifestation.

The Word of God must flow from the ear to the heart. Without reaching the heart it lies dormant and unattended in the mind. If we sit in worship service and simply listen we won't learn. Our listening must be accompanied by an opening of the heart. We must listen by inviting the words to penetrate into our deepest and secret place. We must allow the words to have full consideration before the enemy has time to convict us with some form of doubt. A sermon must be eaten, consumed. This is why the Lord often instructed His champions to eat the words. Our ears are direct channels to the mind, but in Christ we allow the words to flow directly to the heart.

I've been a pastor now for over twenty-eight years and I have come to learn that my story is quite common. So many of us, in the body of Christ, exist without any authority for our daily living. The common language must be spoken so that common people will hear gladly. It is the duty of a pastor to preach and teach with a commitment to reach the heart of every member and to continually provide the "how to" information needed. I have been in worship services when the "Amen's" were shouted loudly, but the people couldn't do much with the sermon after it was over. There was no action agenda given beyond benediction. The first believers called themselves, "Followers of The Way." This was prior to the term "Christian." Those early believers understood that there is certain "way" we are to live. To some degree, I think we have lost that. We have become so intellectual in our theology and faith that maybe we're forgetting the basics.

We have placed so much emphasis on the preached "Word" that we have forgotten the living "Way." Jesus said, "I am the way, the truth and the life." A "way" means a direction; it suggests some form of guidance and instruction. The living Way of God must accompany the preached Word of God.

There are countless millions of Christians who live below the radar of God's authority given to us. They have heard scores of sermons but live in impotence. You know Sister Sarah; she's the best member in the church. You can count on her to volunteer at the drop of a hat. She never misses worship. She prays daily. She pays her tithes and gives generously. She will head a committee or sweep the floor. She is the epitome of a good church member however there is another side to Sister Sarah. She is plagued by indecision, doubt and fear. Her life and the life of her family are in constant turmoil. She sits alone in worship service while her husband and children are absent. The enemy has attacked those that she loves the most. She sits idly by while Satan has his way with them. She prays, but ineffectually, because her faith is steeped in perfunctory ritualism. She thinks that her worship attendance and her ritual of service are enough, but her own fear and doubt cancel out her prayers. The prayers of the righteous do avail much, but a person must truly be righteous and this means to be faithful. A walk in fear will create a darker night. Satan is not bothered by consistent worship attendance and your prayers don't frighten him. He sees there is no manifesting.

POWER TO LIVE is my humble attempt to bridge the gap between church membership and Kingdom Authority. I was deeply affected by Dr. Adrian Rodgers book, KINGDOM AUTHORITY. It was as though his words verified my mission, my ministry, my anointing. I have never attempted to be the best preacher, with oratorical splendor. I've simply attempted to change the lives of all those I could reach. My burning has been to challenge Christians to live better under the umbrella of the authority Christ gave to us. Again, it is the "Way." My commission is to teach people the "Way" to live. Many have been called to the masses, but I have been called to the church. My work, within the Body, is to empower the powerless to manifest God's Word into life application.

For all the holiness and faithfulness of my grandmother, Mary Adkins, a Baptist, she never had any power to live. She had tremendous power to die. On the contrary, my mother, Georgia Adkins, a Roman Catholic, had tremendous power to live. Her power however was not faith-based; it was driven by the desire to achieve. In that, her life was littered with tragedy and pain. My grandmother's life could only be described as a lingering, a hanging around until that "getting up morning." All she thought about was heaven and home. Like Mary and Martha, there needs to be a fusion of the two mindsets. My grandmother somehow construed that there was some kind of sin attached to prosperity and accomplishment. Poverty was somehow justified by the faith. Suffering was expected and ordinary. My mother simply pressed ahead with what she had, which was not much. She did not have an essential spiritual foundation but pressed ahead with a voracious drive to succeed. Both loved the Lord and both had hope. But neither had, nor even understood the potential of the authority Christ gave to us. Much of their trouble and trial was avoidable through the power that was available. However neither recognized nor even conceived of such authority. One waited to die and another fought to live.

Jesus came not only to redeem us from our sins, but He also came to empower us for living. He declared in the Gospel of John that the mission of the thief was theft, death and destruction, but He had come that we might have life (eternal and temporal), more abundantly. I stand on that premise! This is not pie in the sky religion, but power-based living through God's Holy Word and according to His Holy Way.

CHAPTER ONE

LE BON VIE (THE GOOD LIFE)

The French like to say "Le Bon Vie," translated "the good life." This expression suggests the quality of life itself. It does not necessarily reference opulent and affluent life, but a manner of good living. It is also utilized as an expression of thanksgiving, often used in toasting, relating to an appreciation for living.

As Macbeth comes to a close, he is seen in the castle of Dunsinane, surrounded by some of his soldiers. Macbeth has come to power through brute force and the loss of many lives. His sins are catching up with him and he is besieged in his castle. He is told that Lady Macbeth is now dead. Then he breaks forth into the following, "Life's but a walking shadow; a poor player, that struts and frets his hour upon the stage. And then is heard no more; it is a tale told by an idiot, full of sound and fury, signifying nothing." Others have belittled life as well. E.V. Cooke said life is a hollow bubble. Robert Browning said life is an empty dream. Isaac Watts described life as a long tragedy and Shakespeare called it a walking shadow. Even Augustine, one our greatest theologian's pondered life when he asked, "Is life a living death or a dying life?"

Allow me to affirm, life is a gift from God. It is His creation and comes only through His divine ordination, therefore it is to be cherished and deeply appreciated. As believers we know that Christ called us to the highest rung of the ladder when announced in John 10:10 (KJV), "The thief cometh not, but for to steal, and to kill, and to destroy: I am come that they might have life, and that they might have it more abundantly."

Jesus' entry into history was for, in part, the establishment of life's purpose. Jesus came to show us how to live life. Here in the same breath, Jesus talks about thievery, death and destruction and abundant life. Jesus somehow interlocks this connection between abundant life and a destroying, killing "thief." The thief is not described as a robber. What is the difference? A robber holds you up to your face. A robber steals from you openly by force. A thief is one that steals from you secretly. A thief wants to keep you in ignorance of his thievery. Jesus is telling us that there is a thief that wants to keep you from the knowledge of the fact that you are being stolen from.

Just a thought: The Christian life must exemplify successful living.

Jesus promises us an abundant life. Abundant translates to living above the mundane and mediocre, above the ordinary; a life of excellence, superfluous; superior in quality. There is however a culprit who's mission is to steal, kill and destroy this extraordinary living, Satan. Living under his threat does not detour our mission to live successfully. In the Purpose Driven Life, Rick Warren wrote, "If I asked you how you picture life, what image would come to your mind? That image is your life metaphor. It's your description of how life works and what you expect from it. It determines your expectations, your values, your relationships, your goals, and your priorities." In other words, life is what we will make it to be. How the Christian perceives his or her life is the foundation of their hope. The sad reality is that so many people who profess Christ as Lord live horrendous lives. Why? Through my years of ministry and serving the Lord's people I've come to the conclusion that there are those in the Body of Christ that have not learned to manifest God's Word into their living. They hear the Word but cannot transform it into daily action. "Sermon-hearers" live empty shallow lives because the word they hear has no true value for living. It is akin to listening to a well-told story and appreciating the story for the story's sake. These people may appreciate the author for his or her scholarship and excellent writing style, but they just don't get it. The story has been cynically listened to and analyzed intellectually but the stream of conscious and the heart of the story have not taken hold. "Sermon-doers" take to heart the words and transform them into action agendas.

Church and worship services have become perfunctory ritualism for some. They never get to the heart of the matter, which is Jesus. Therefore their living is always left wanting and unfulfilled. No one can truly enjoy life until they find their proper place with God. The writer of Hebrews challenges us to let some things go, "Therefore, since we are surrounded by such a huge crowd of witnesses to the life of faith, let us strip off every weight that slows us down, especially the sin that so easily hinders our progress. And let us run with endurance the race that God has set before us. We do this by keeping our eyes on Jesus, on whom our faith depends from start to finish. He was willing to die a shameful death on the cross because of the joy he knew would be his afterward. Now he is seated in the place of highest honor beside God's throne in heaven." (Hebrews 12:1, 2 NLT) James writes in 1:17, "Every good and perfect gift comes from the Father." Life is the ultimate gift. Christian maturity may be summed up in how we appreciate the gift of life. We know there will be times of trial and tribulation however our mindset is such that we rebound instantly. God desires success for you and troubles can not stop you, they can only detour you.

Another thought: Maybe it's time to grow up!

Aristotle says there are three tenses to a person's life; what he is, what he has become, and what he is becoming. There are three stages of Christian development; spiritual infancy, spiritual adolescence and spiritual maturity. Where are you today? At what stage are you in your growth as a believer? Plants grow deeper before they grow taller and we as believers develop much the same. As we grow spiritually we become taller and become more mature. We are called to recognize who we are, what we are, and whose we are. That recognition itself clarifies our "becoming." Power for living is delivered at the level of spiritual maturity. Chronological age is insignificant, only the maturation of the believer matters.

I remember as a child, my mother constantly saying to me, "grow-up." There were instances when I injured myself and began to cry, my mother would urge me to be a "little man" and soak up the tears. There were other cases of hurt, rejection and even discrimination and my mother would say, "It's just a lesson of life, deal with it." To some my mother may seem harsh, but her mission was to grow a boy into a man. As a pastor I see my role to grow spiritual infants into mature power-based believers. I will address "power" and its sometime misunderstanding in a subsequent chapter.

Power-based believers live life to the fullest of their potential through Christ Jesus. The "good life" is established when effectual power is realized. The authority that Christ gave us is to be utilized in our daily living. Jesus taught us in Matthew 18:18, 19, "Verily I say unto you, whatsoever ye shall bind on earth shall be bound in heaven: and whatsoever ye shall loose on earth shall be loosed in heaven. Again I say unto you, that if two of you shall agree on earth as touching any thing that they shall ask, it shall be done for them of my Father which is in heaven." When we accept Jesus as Lord and Savior we are given power and authority, enabling us to live life as a child of God. The power and authority are there from the very beginning, but our spiritual immaturity does not realize there potency or availability. Someone said, "You can have all the money in the world in a bank, but if you don't write a check it's useless."

Pay attention: The secret is the keys!

Matthew 16:19 (KJV) reports Jesus as saying we have the keys of the kingdom. Keys represent authority. The janitor at our church likes to walk around with his keys, jingling them. He knows he has the authority to unlock every door in the facility at his own discretion. A door is a barrier, an obstacle, but once you possess the key it no longer hinders you. We possess the keys of the kingdom, we have authority. The power of heaven binds what we bind. The power of heaven looses what we loose. This is power-based living. The divine implication is that we must perform an earthly function before there is a heavenly action. We must address the issues that thwart our successful living and good life. Too many Christians live powerless lives far below the radar of God's provision. A humorous story was told about a family that, well let's say, were not too bright. A man, apparently the father and husband, was outside the car door with a coat hanger attempting to unlock the car because he left his keys inside. Inside the car was his wife and children cheering him on to successfully negotiate the hanger over the door lock to free them. Seems unlikely, but it is possible. Christians do the same. The keys of power and authority are only a reach away. Yet, some of us are looking for someone else to free us.

I am amazed with the fervor surrounding Feng Shui, the Oriental art of successful living by design. Its premise is that when you place certain things in their proper place the forces of harmony will align themselves and create a successful environment. The sad note here is that some Christians will give Feng Shui a try, attempting to arrange their homes for health and happiness. With proper placement in Jesus Christ all hope is realized. The promises are revealed and the authority is given. Jesus called his disciples to Him to give them authority. They received his authority because of their relationship or placement, with Jesus. Our Authority is based solely on our relationship and placement with Jesus. That is why we must maintain our positioning. Apart from Christ we are nothing, powerless and hopeless. The "good life" is the goal of every believer; it is the quintessence of witness and testimony. Try it, you just may like it.

Reflection: We are challenged to live the "good life." Our living must be exemplary of our belief and therefore a living epistle to the world. What good is it for us to proclaim the power of Christ and not live the power? For too long the church has neglected to teach a power-based concept of Christian living and testimony, all for the sake of vain glory. The community of faith must grow to the comprehension that part of Jesus' mission was for us to have a better life through Him.

PowerPoints!

- **Life is a gift from God; live like it.**
- **Know that the thief is continually stealing from you.**
- **Find your proper place with God.**
- **Teach yourself to rebound from trial and tribulation.**
- **Like a boxer, learn to roll with life's punches.**
- **Speak the good things and believe them.**

CHAPTER TWO

POWER TO LIVE

I
f we consider faith as a verb and not as a noun we will come closer to the purpose of faith in action. For those that regard faith as a noun, there is no action required, therefore, faith becomes something religious and admired instead of performed. For most of my Christian life I have been prepared for heaven and home. I've heard sermon after sermon about "gittin up mornings" and "crossing over Jordan." I too, wait that day when I'll see my Master's face, but for right now, the people of God need to know how to live victoriously.

West Africans tell the story that the gazelle wakes each morning with one thought, that they must outrun the fastest lion. The lion wakes up each day with a similar thought, that they must outrun the slowest gazelle. Believer's who understand that God gives us power to live, run fast. Unbelievers who are slow to realize their own kingdom authority run slow and therefore, easily devoured.

Why do so many Christians live below their privileged positions? I say miseducation, misrepresentation and misunderstanding of God's will and purpose for us. The essential prerequisite for knowing the will of God is our positive disposition toward it. Jesus said in John 7:17 (NASB), "If anyone is willing to do His will, he will know of the teaching, whether it is of God or whether I speak from Myself." Disobedience affects discernment. Getting your own way excludes God's Way. A true disciple of Jesus glorifies the Lord and finds his or her affirmation through that and that alone. Power to live comes through the knowledge of God's will and purpose for us.

For centuries people believed that Aristotle was right when he said that the heavier an object, the faster it would fall to earth. Aristotle was regarded as the greatest thinker of all time, and surely he would not be wrong. Anyone, of course, could have taken two objects; one heavy and one light, and dropped them from a great height to see whether or not the heavier object landed first. But no one did until nearly 2,000 years after Aristotle's death. In 1589 Galileo summoned learned professors to the base of the Leaning Tower of Pisa. Then he went to the top and pushed off a ten- pound and a one-pound weight. Both landed at the same instant. The power of belief was so strong that the professors denied their eyesight. They continued to say Aristotle was right.

Why live below your privileged position? Neil T. Anderson writes in his book, FINDING GOD'S WILL, "Suppose you are a prostitute. One day you hear that the king has decreed that all prostitutes are forgiven. That would be great news; however, it would not necessarily change your behavior or your self-perception." You may shout for a while and dance in the streets for a minute, but at the end of all the rejoicing you would still be a prostitute, according to your condition. You would understand yourself to be nothing more than a forgiven prostitute. But suppose the king not only forgave you, but he made you his bride. Now you are a queen. Would that change your perception of yourself? Knowing that you are now the queen and married to the king would change your behavior. You would not continue to live as a prostitute now that you are a queen.

Real and true affirmation comes through the process of corrected behavior and perception. Lean on the fact that Jesus affirms you through correction. Listen to the words of 1 Peter 2:9 (KJV), "But ye are a chosen generation, a royal priesthood, an holy nation, a peculiar people; that ye should shew forth the praises of him who hath called you out of darkness into his marvelous light." The Apostle Paul wrote in Ephesians 1:18 (NASB), "I pray that the eyes of your heart may be enlightened, so that you will know what is the hope of His calling, what are the riches of the glory of His inheritance in the saints."

Jesus meets all our needs according to His riches in glory. Your privilege and purpose are complete in and through Him. We are not followers of a historical Jesus, but we are believers in a Risen Savior. Because He is still alive we are duty-bound to manifest his life into our own living. We just don't celebrate and commemorate, but we validate through our victorious living in Him.

Question: Are you ready to utilize your power?

I am amazed at the numbers of people that fill our pews every Sunday that are replete with weakness, doubt and fear. Like Isaiah, I sometimes question, "Have they heard our report?" Further study is needed, more than this humble writer can attain, as to why so many Christians live as victims rather than victors. I know the simple answer, but that does not seem to suffice. I can only continue to suggest that there is a better way to live. It appears that within the body, there is some notion that the word "power" is offensive and obtrusive to the gospels. The word "power" in the New Testament comes from two Greek root words, *dunamis* and *exousia*. When Jesus said, "All power is given unto me in heaven and in earth," the word used is *exousia*. It means authority. Therefore, the Lord actually said, "All authority is given unto me." "At the name of Jesus every knee should bow, of things in heaven, and things in earth, and things under the earth; and that every tongue should confess that Jesus Christ is Lord." (Philippians 2:10, 11, KJV)

I believe that most of us understand that when you have authority, you have power. Consider this analogy. In Mexico City a number of Boy Scouts were trying to cross the Avenue Reforma, a great boulevard in the heart of the city. It was during rush hour and the traffic was bumper to bumper. The boys made it halfway across the broad street and took refuge on the esplanade in the street's center. There, in the middle of the street, is a tall special chair, high on a pedestal where the traffic officer would raise his right hand and all the powerful speeding automobiles would screech to a halt. That pedestal is a seat of authority and all the motorists understood that. About this time, a slight accident occurred nearby and the officer left his place to investigate. While he was arguing with the motorist, one of the boy Scouts stepped up on the pedestal and raised his right hand. Instantly, cars began to grind to a halt. All the motorists could clearly see that the hand, which was raised in the air, was the hand of a young boy, but it did not matter. The motorists recognized that the boy was sitting in the place of authority. That seat represented the government of Mexico and it did not matter whose hand it was, what mattered was that the young boy was sitting in the seat of authority.

Here's a thought: Every true believer sits in the seat of authority!

The greatest power in the universe stands behind the believer. The believer has the seat of authority regardless of his or her stature or age. When Jesus said, "All authority has been given unto me in heaven and in earth," and then in the next verse said, "Go ye therefore," He was talking to the disciples. He was addressing His words to the church. He was saying, "I have the authority and I delegate that authority to you. Go ye therefore and preach the Gospel." God Himself is the force behind the authority. The authority possessed by the believer is greater than any power of an enemy.

Let's pause and pray right here, God I pray that you open their eyes so that they may see more than their problem, more than their predicament, more than their pain, more than their dismay, more than their fear, more than their worry, more than their doubt, more than their hurt, and more than their disillusion. God let them see that they are not alone. Let them know and understand that if you are for us, who can be against us? Let them know that I have yet to see the righteous forsaken, nor his seed begging bread. Accomplish in them the essentials of faith and place them in the bosom of your love and protection. We declare right now that no force, internal or external, mental or spiritual, physiological, financial, organizational or interpersonal shall raise its ugly head against us. In the name of Jesus we pray, AMEN.

Jesus came to the earth and recognized our sin. He investigated our circumstances. He realized our guilt. He knew our despair. He weighed our burdens and witnessed our weaknesses, but most importantly He visualized our destiny. His life became the solution to our problems, to establish a manner by which we could overcome the world. Jesus stepped into our shoes, knowing that there was a death penalty upon us that lingered from Adam and Eve. Therefore He took the necessary steps that redeemed us through His own death. It was not that He wanted to suffer, but that He chose to suffer in our place. Through all of this we are to rise upon this vicarious suffering and establish within our own living a pattern of faith that overcomes all obstacles.

Jesus came to the earth on a three-fold mission: to redeem us from our sins, receive new life in Him and undo the works of the enemy. Our charge is to accomplish the task of victorious living. Redemption has been completed through the act of atonement. Eternal life is offered to those who believe. Satan is completely corrected by the victory over death and the grave. Jesus died on the cross for our sins, but He also came to give us life. We have been rescued from the domain of darkness and transferred by God into the kingdom of His beloved Son.

Question: Do you know how to have success through Christ?

It is important that we clearly understand an important concept of our faith. We are to make the most of every opportunity given to us. We must be the best we can be at every present assignment, and stay there until God calls you elsewhere. In other words, we must bloom wherever we are planted. We are to succeed and never succumb. We glorify God by manifesting His presence and we do that when we bear the fruit of successful living in and through Him. "My Father is glorified by this, that you bear much fruit, and so prove to be my disciples (John 15:8, NASB)." Our responsibility is not just to celebrate and commemorate His glorious victory of death and the grave. Ours is the task to begin our own accomplishments and set in motion the process of glorifying Him in our living. God's glory is the external manifestation of His being. The glory of God must be manifested in us as we dwell in the earth. His goodness must shine through us. The plan of salvation was realized by the empty tomb, but the process of glorification in us begins with our acknowledgment that we are in debt to Him because of His payment on Calvary. As long as there is a cross there is sin, but with an empty tomb there is redemption.

"Now faith is the substance of things hoped for, the evidence of things not seen." Hebrews 11:1 (KJV) is the only definition of faith in the Scriptures. If we are going to move into God's abundance we must understand that definition. The writer of Hebrews describes faith as "the substance of things hoped for." However, the word in the Greek has in it the sense of an action. To use the word "substance" implies the virtue of a noun instead of a verb.

In a seminary mission's class, Herbert Jackson told how, as a new missionary, he was assigned a car that would not start without a push. After pondering his problem, he devised a plan. He went to the school near his home, got permission to take some children out of class, and had them push his car off. As he made his rounds, he would either park on a hill or leave the engine running. He used this ingenious procedure for two years. Ill health forced the Jackson family to leave, and a new missionary came to that station. When Jackson proudly began to explain his arrangement for getting the car started, the new man began looking under the hood. Before the explanation was complete, the new missionary interrupted, "Why, Dr. Jackson, I believe the only trouble is this loose cable." He gave the cable a twist, stepped into the car, pushed the switch, and to Jackson's astonishment, the engine roared to life. For two years needless trouble had become routine. The power was there all the time. Only a loose connection kept Jackson from putting that power to work.

Faithful living is power-connected living. God's people must lift up their heads and move into an awareness of the charge given to us to live this life more abundantly. The thief's mission is to rob us, kill us, steal from us and if possible, destroy us. Make the choice to disappoint him. Henry Blackaby, the author of EXPERIENCING GOD writes: "We should attempt things so great that they are doomed to failure unless God intervenes."

Reflection: The power that Christ gives us has always been available to us. It is up to us to utilize it. To be in Christ without any power is to be like a Ferrari sports car without gasoline. Useless!

PowerPoints!

- **Real faith requires action. I will act.**
- **I have jurisdictional authority, I will exercise it.**
- **I am privileged. I will live like it.**

- If I am going to talk like a Christian, I need to take authority like one.
- Faithful living is power-connected living.
- I must remember, "I am better and stronger than even I think."

CHAPTER THREE

POWER TO AGGRESSIVELY MOVE TOWARD YOUR JOY

John 16: 20 – 24 (KJV) records Jesus saying, "Verily, verily, I say unto you, that ye shall weep and lament, but the world shall rejoice: and ye shall be sorrowful, but your sorrow shall be turned into joy. A woman when she is in travail hath sorrow, because her hour is come: but as soon as she is delivered of the child, she remembereth no more the anguish, for joy that a man is born into the world. And ye now therefore have sorrow: but I will see you again, and your heart shall rejoice, and your joy no man taketh from you. And in that day ye shall ask me nothing. Verily, verily, I say unto you, whatsoever ye shall ask the Father in my name, he will give it you. Hitherto have ye asked nothing in my name: ask, and ye shall receive, that your joy may be full."

Here's a suggestion: Picture joy as a pool, dive in!

For power-filled living let's take a plunge into the pool called "joy." We are not only going to claim our joy, but we are going to aggressively seek after it! Joy is a Fruit of the Spirit as found in Galatians 5:22-23 (NIV): "But the fruit of the Spirit is love, joy, peace, patience, kindness, goodness, faithfulness, gentleness and self-control." It is safe to say that joy is one of the most elusive fruits for us as believers. It is not a very popular fruit and doesn't get near enough use today. Part of the problem is that joy is often misunderstood. We tend to equate "happiness" with joy but they differ because they each come from a different source. One comes from the world around me. The other originates directly from the Spirit of the Living God inside me. Happiness is conditioned by and often dependent upon what is happening to me. Joy, on the other hand, throbs throughout Scripture as a profound, compelling quality of life that transcends the events and disasters which may oppress God's people. Joy is a divine dimension of living that is not shackled by circumstances. The Hebrew definition of joy means, "To leap or spin around with pleasure." In the New Testament the word refers to "gladness, bliss and celebration." To have the fruit of joy ripen in our lives is to recognize the journey involved in getting there. It takes time, diligence, patience, and hard work to make a grapevine produce grapes. There must even be an aggressive move toward it.

Question: Do you know the joy busters?

Fruit is not instantaneous because it has to overcome weather, bugs, weeds, poor soil and neglect. If we want to see this fruit ripen in our lives, we desperately need the Holy Ghost to prune away whatever it is that hinders our joy and then empower us to make some choices that move us closer to a lifestyle of rejoicing. We need to guard against three common joy busters that harm us. Before Paul wrote to the church at Galatia about the Fruit of the Spirit in chapter 5, he asked a very penetrating question in Galatians 4:15 (NIV), says, "Where, then is that joyful and grateful spirit you felt then?" Or to put it another way, "What has happened to all your joy?" That question needs to be asked in the church today. What has happened to all your joy?

Allow me to identify three joy busters:

1. Unsatisfied expectations. Do you ever feel like you're just going through some joyless routines in life? If the truth were known some of us are discontent with the way our lives are progressing. It could be that your expectations for your marriage have not been met. Or, maybe your kids aren't living like they should. Perhaps you don't have everything you want, a larger home, a nicer car, and a better job. I'm convinced that a spirit of discontentment can rob many of us of our joy. Listen to how Paul discovered the secret of

being content with what God had given him in Philippians 4:12 (NIV), "I know what it is to be in need, and I know what it is to have plenty. I have learned the secret of being content in any and every situation, whether well fed or hungry, whether living in plenty or in want." I find it interesting to note that Paul calls contentment a "secret." There's a mystery about it. He also had to learn how to live with unsatisfied expectations. Likewise, we must learn to live with plenty or with little. Contentment doesn't come when we have everything we want but when we want everything we have.

2. Unresolved conflict. Our joy evaporates when we allow conflict between ourselves and other people to go on. When someone's offense against us occupies our mental and emotional attention, we have little leftover for the Lord. Anger clouds the eyes of our heart and obscures our view of God, draining away our joy. Hebrews 12:14-15 (NIV) challenges us to not allow relational ruptures to fester because bitterness can set in,

"Make every effort to live in peace with all men and to be holy; without holiness no one will see the Lord. See to it that no one misses the grace of God and that no bitter root grows up to cause trouble and defile many." Don't be itemizing other people's mess-ups. If you're still itemizing people's mess-ups, the fruit of joy will be squashed in your life. Paul recognizes the link between joy and unity in Philippians 2:2 (NIV), "Then make my joy complete by being like-minded, having the same love, being one in spirit and of one mind."

3. Unconfessed sin. This third joy buster is perhaps responsible for chasing more joy out of lives than any other. Guilt can gut your joy faster than anything I know. Sin can send joy far away. David understood this very well when he attempted to ignore the promptings of the Spirit. Take a look at Psalm 32:1-5 (NLT), "Oh, what joy for those whose rebellion is forgiven, whose sin is put out of sight! Yes, what joy for those whose record the LORD has cleared of sin, whose lives are lived in complete honesty! When I refused to confess my sin, I was weak and miserable, and I groaned all day long. Day and night your hand of discipline was heavy

on me. My strength evaporated like water in the summer heat. Finally, I confessed all my sins to you and stopped trying to hide them. I said to myself, "I will confess my rebellion to the LORD." And you forgave me! All my guilt is gone." Look at how this Psalm ends. After David owns his sin, his joy returns, "So rejoice in the LORD and be glad, all you who obey him! Shout for joy, all you whose hearts are pure!" (Psalm 32:11, NIV)

Do you get it? He was not able to rejoice and experience the joy of the Lord until he confessed his sins! That is very similar to what David wrote in Psalm 51:7-8 (NIV), "Cleanse me with hyssop, and I will be clean; wash me, and I will be whiter than snow. Let me hear joy and gladness; let the bones you have crushed rejoice." Here comes the good news. The Lord God Himself breaks out in song when you discover your joy. Consider Zephaniah 3:17 (NIV), "The LORD your God is with you, he is mighty to save. He will take great delight in you, he will quiet you with his love, he will rejoice over you with singing." Psalm 104:31 (NIV) says, "May the glory of the LORD endure forever; may the LORD rejoice in his works." Isaiah 65:18-19 (NIV): "But be glad and rejoice forever in what I will create, for I will create Jerusalem to be a delight and its people a joy. I will rejoice over Jerusalem and take delight in my people…" You cannot rejoice until you first establish your joy!

Question: Does your appearance say to the world, you have joy?

The German philosopher and skeptic Nietzsche said, "I would believe in their salvation if they looked a little more like people who have been saved." The extrinsic should compliment the intrinsic. Every believer of Christ must know that our demeanor is part of our witness. Absence of outward joy is an indication of an inward absence. With aggression we must seek and establish the joyful in us. It is our knowledge of what Jesus has done for us that establishes this joy. Joseph Haydn, the great composer was asked why his church music was so cheerful, he replied, "When I think upon God, my heart is so full of joy that the notes dance and leap, as it were, from my pen, and since God has given me a cheerful heart it will be pardoned men that I serve Him with a cheerful spirit." People that establish joy are infectious. To be around them makes one grow in their personal joy. This is the true nature of the believer, to be that infectious joyful saint of God that rejoices continually and allows their light to shine brightly. Billy Graham said in his message "Saved or Lost" in Texas in 1965. "One of the fruits of the Spirit is joy. You might not be able to work up joy yourself, but God the Holy Spirit living inside of you can produce this joy supernaturally, and a Christian is to have joy."

He went on to say, "But a Christian is to have joy. That's one of the great characteristics of the Christian is the joy that we have, and if you don't have this joy and if you don't have this peace that Christ gives, you had better search your heart and find out if you really know Christ."

It seems dichotomous to think of aggression with joy. However it is time that the body of Christ becomes more aggressive. Satan is not taking a vacation and it appears that he's working harder than we are. There are so many things that complicate our living and challenge our joy. His attacks are more sophisticated and clever. He is not that cartoon character with a pitchfork and tail, but rather appears to be politically correct and even rational. He has come out of the Garden of Eden and has donned a tuxedo. With stealth he approaches us with ideas of materialism and vain glory, but what we end up with is a bankrupted spirit. To aggressively move toward our joy we must first be willing to utilize the power and authority, placing Satan and his cohorts under our feet. We cannot sit and wait for something to happen, bur rather stand, put our feet down, show no mercy and seize our victory. "When the LORD thy God shall bring thee into the land whither thou goest to possess it, and hath cast out many nations before thee, the Hittites, and the Girgashites, and the Amorites, and the Canaanites, and the Perizzites, and the Hivites, and the Jebusites, seven nations greater and mightier than thou; And when the LORD thy God shall deliver them before thee; thou shalt smite them, and utterly destroy them; thou shalt make no covenant with them, nor shew mercy unto them." (Deuteronomy 7: 1, 2 KJV) Jesus said to us in Luke 10:19 (KJV), "Behold, I give unto you power to tread on serpents and scorpions, and over all the power of the enemy: and nothing shall by any means hurt you."

To establish your joy you must utilize His power. The writer of Hebrews (10: 19-23, KJV) tells us that the blood of Jesus gives us might, "Having therefore, brethren, boldness to enter into the holiest by the blood of Jesus,

By a new and living way, which he hath consecrated for us, through the veil, that is to say, his flesh; And having an high priest over the house of God; Let us draw near with a true heart in full assurance of faith, having our hearts sprinkled from an evil conscience, and our bodies washed with pure water. Let us hold fast the profession of our faith without wavering; (for he is faithful that promised)." Philippians 2: 9 – 11 (KJV) teaches us that by the Name of Jesus we have authority, "Wherefore God also hath highly exalted him, and given him a name which is above every name: That at the name of Jesus every knee should bow, of things in heaven, and things in earth, and things under the earth; And that every tongue should confess that Jesus Christ is Lord, to the glory of God the Father."

Zig Ziglar tells the story of boy that went with his mother to the old general store. He liked to sneak away from his mother and when no one was looking he would dip his finger into the large barrel of molasses. The storekeeper caught him doing this and decided to teach the boy a lesson. He picked up the boy by his britches and dunked him head first into the barrel of molasses and then set him out on the front porch of the store. But instead of crying the boy was out there praying, "God, give me the tongue to equal this opportunity." The power that God gives us comes through opportunity in Him. However, this power of God will come only to the believer that has established God's presence. When the presence is realized the manifestation of ability is reckoned. Now we speak boldly, that is with aggression, to the establishment of our joy. The presence and the fruit of the spirit (joy) work together. Seek His presence to establish your power!

Reflection: There was a time in my life when I was deeply depressed. Nothing or no one seemed capable of giving me joy. It was only when I truly found Jesus Christ that I found and established my joy. Since that day I have maintained it through adversity and pain. This joy that I have, the world didn't give it to me, and therefore the world cannot take it away from me!

PowerPoints!

- Joy must be established. Establish it!
- Joy must be maintained. Maintain it!
- Joy must be fought for. Fight for it!
- Recognize Satan's devices and overcome them.
- Wear your joy daily.
- Utilize your authority and power. Believe in them!

CHAPTER FOUR

GOD'S INCOMPARABLE POWER IN US

The Apostle Paul writes to Ephesus, "And what is the exceeding greatness of his power to us-ward who believe, according to the working of his mighty power, which he wrought in Christ, when he raised him from the dead, and set him at his own right hand in the heavenly places. Now unto him that is able to do exceeding abundantly above all that we ask or think, according to the power that worketh in us." (Ephesians 1:19,20; 3:20 KJV)

Here is a thought: You are rich and powerful!

Jesus Christ left behind for true believers a rich inheritance. Besides the heavenly inheritance prepared for the saints, there is a present inheritance in the saints. There is a glory in this inheritance, riches of glory, rendering the Christian more excellent and more truly honorable than all others. What is the exceeding greatness of God's power towards those who believe? The answer comes to those who truly believe in the all-sufficiency of God, and the omnipotence of divine grace. 2 Corinthians 12:9 (KJV) reports God saying to the Apostle Paul, "My grace is sufficient for thee: for my strength is made perfect in weakness. Most gladly therefore will I rather glory in my infirmities, that the power of Christ may rest upon me."

Jesus performed miracles as the Son of Man, which was in the flesh of a man. Many would prefer to see Him only in the capacity as Son of God therefore seeing those miracles as from His heavenly power. However,

His announcement to us that "greater works" we would do signified the concept of earthly authority given to us. In other words He said, as you see me do, so can you. It is the power of God working in us that enables us. The same power that God exerts towards His people is the same power by which he raised Christ from the dead. "No one can know what anyone else is really thinking except that person alone and no one can know God's thoughts except God's own Spirit. And God has actually given us his Spirit (not the world's spirit) so we can know the wonderful things God has freely given us." (1 Corinthians 2:11, 12, NLT) This is the great proof of the truth of the gospel to the world. But the truth of this power is proven by our own sanctification, and rising from the death of our sins. The power that God exerts towards us is affirmed by the inward power of sanctification working within us. Jesus said in John 17:17-19 (KJV), "Sanctify them through thy truth: thy word is truth. As thou hast sent me into the world, even so have I also sent them into the world? And for their sakes I sanctify myself, that they also might be sanctified through the truth." We are sanctified by the truth of a divine reality. Having been raised from the dead, Christ is now the supreme head of the church, the ultimate authority over the world. Jesus told the apostles that once they understood who He really was they would never suffer lack again. "For all who are led by the Spirit of God are children of God. So you should not be like cowering, fearful slaves. You should behave instead like God's very own children, adopted into his family--calling him 'Father, dear Father.' For his Holy Spirit speaks to us deep in our heart and tells us that we are God's children." (Romans 8:14-16, TLB)

The gifted orator William Jennings Bryan is recorded having said, "I have observed the power of the watermelon seed. It has the power of drawing from the ground and through itself 200,000 times its weight. When you can tell me how it takes this material and out of it colors an outside surface beyond the imitation of art, and then forms inside of it a white rind and within that again a red heart, thickly inlaid with black seeds, each one of which in turn is capable of drawing through itself 200,000 times its weight, when you can explain to me the mystery of a watermelon, you can ask me to explain the mystery of God." Like Bryan, I can see the mysteries of God and become awestruck by there power. We are like that watermelon seed. Our lives begin as infinitesimal microorganisms, yet we develop into erect human beings with distinct features and attributes.

Question: Don't you think it's time we woke up?

Paul writes to the saints at Rome in the thirteenth chapter, "And that, knowing the time, that now it is high time to awake out of sleep: for now is our salvation nearer than when we believed. The night is far spent, the day is at hand: let us therefore cast off the works of darkness, and let us put on the armor of light. Let us walk honestly, as in the day not in rioting and drunkenness, not in chambering and wantonness, not in strife and envying. But put ye on the Lord Jesus Christ, and make not provision for the flesh, to fulfill the lusts thereof."

There is a tremendous inference in the Bible concerning the word "wait." Waiting on the Lord is the necessity of faith. Determining that God will deliver in God's due time is the process of faith. As you'll read in a later chapter, waiting, therefore, is the product of faith. Waiting, however, is not the totality of the believer's opportunity in Christ. There is an authority over the present. There is an authority over your present condition, over your present finances, over your present problems. I'm talking about some "right-now stuff." Jesus gives us might to effectuate change in our lives. This might becomes the believer's authority. John Ortberg writes, "Most people I know love to hear stories and images about the powerful God we serve. But here is the problem: That information alone is not sufficient enough to create courageous human beings. I can receive much information designed to assure me that God's power is sufficient. But the information alone does not transform the human heart and character. In order for such a transformation to take place, certain actions and experiences are required."

After Moses had died, and the children of Israel wondered if God would continue to take care of them, they came to the River Jordan. God had promised the people that He would make a way for them. The scripture stated, "When the soles of the feet of the priests who bear the ark of the Lord, the Lord of all the earth, rest in the waters of the Jordan, the waters of the Jordan flowing from above shall be cut off; they shall stand in a single heap." To experience the power and awesomeness of God is worth the risk. As I explained earlier, faith is having the guts to take the risk. When I took the risk of giving generously, tithing, I realized that God's promise is true. He will take care of me and bless me abundantly. But the first time I gave my tithe, it was a risk. I put my wife Linda and the children at risk. My financial stability was at risk. My security was at risk. I took the risk, an act of faith, trusting God's Word. And God showed me His favor for my trust in Him.

Here's a thought: You do not have to take what the enemy is putting on you!

When I think about my past life I quickly realize that only the power of God could have kept me. There were so many occasions for my destruction, yet the Lord Jesus loved me even though I was in sin. Foolishly adrift in the world, I survived by the stored prayers of those who loved me. The awesomeness of God's incomparable power was directed towards me by the power of prayer. It is easy for me to now envisage my predicament. With clarity I completely understand that His power was there to save me from me. And he will save you from you! His power works in so many arenas, inside you, outside you, without you and because of you. This power becomes most effectual when it becomes centered within you. Paul wrote to the Romans that any present suffering cannot be compared to the glory of God that shall be revealed in us. While we wait on God in faith, God is waiting on us to reveal His power in us. God wants the enemy and prince of this world to see His power working in you. Satan is well aware of God's power. He is not aware of yours. Now unto him that is able to do exceeding abundantly above all that we ask or think, according to the power that worketh in us. Ephesians 1:19, 20; 3:20 (KJV)

Reflection: Too many of us wait on God to deliver us when sometimes the power of God that is already at work in us is sufficient. Moses stood gazing at a sea in front of him with mountains on each side and Pharaoh coming from behind to destroy him and his people. While Moses was asking God to help and deliver, God asked Moses, "What's that in your hand?" In other words, what have I already given you? What has God already given you?

PowerPoints!

- I have already inherited my power to live, I am an heir!
- Waiting on the Lord is the necessity of faith.
- All my outward power comes from my inward spiritual power.
- Taking a risk is not always foolish, sometimes it's faithful.
- God hears my prayer, but Satan needs to know my power.
- Stand offensively, not defensively.
- Show no mercy to a merciless enemy.

CHAPTER FIVE

THE POWER OF WHAT WE SPEAK AND SAY

It is my desire that an understanding is reached through this book. You must know that whatever is in your heart will find a way of expressing itself through your mouth. The enemy blinds the eye of faith and opens the mouth of nullification and doubt. A soul under Satan's power, and led captive by him, is blind to the things of God, and dumb at the throne of grace; sees nothing, and says nothing to the purpose. Our purposes in life must be spoken to. We must say something to address the purpose. The rule of life is, "We speak what we believe." There is a connection between our mouth and our heart. Our text says, "for out of the abundance of the heart the mouth speaketh." You cannot separate one from the other. The mouth is like a faucet that lets out what already is inside our hearts. If your heart is filled with the Word of God, if you are standing in faith on what God's Word says, then that faith will be expressed out of your mouth. However, if your soul is under the control of the enemy, you are dumb (meaning you cannot speak with authority) before the throne of grace.

Jesus says in Matthew 12: 34 –37 (KJV), "O generation of vipers, how can ye, being evil, speak good things? for out of the abundance of the heart the mouth speaketh. A good man out of the good treasure of the heart bringeth forth good things: and an evil man out of the evil treasure bringeth forth evil things. But I say unto you, that every idle word that men shall speak, they shall give account thereof in the day of judgment. For by thy words thou shalt be justified, and by thy words thou shalt be condemned."

People that are filled with unbelief and fear are bound by spiritual strongholds that manifest themselves by coming forth out of the mouth. The mouth is the center of spiritual warfare for the universe. The enemy attacks us through the mind with thought grenades. Some people cannot be blessed because they think beyond their blessing! Our confidence in what we sometimes think is our greatest weakness. We should have more confidence in the conviction of our hearts, which is our soul. The enemy works to establish a stronghold in our lives through our thought processes. He wants his evil thoughts to capture our hearts. He wants those thoughts to take root inside of us. He wants them to be something that we believe in, more so than God. If Satan can capture your heart, then he will have control of your mouth! Once the heart is captured, the mouth will speak the things of the heart. The bible teaches us that the mouth speaks out of the abundance of the heart.

Question: What's in your heart today?

The more the mouth confesses the presence of the stronghold, the more the stronghold grips and controls the person. For this purpose we need to examine the process of confession. The word most often used in the New Testament for confession is *homologeo*. It essentially means to speak what is truly believed within, a confession of what's inside, to speak the convictions of what a person truly believes. When we hear the word confession in relationship to God's Word we errantly think of confessing sin, iniquity, and transgression. That is the negative connotation of the word. But on the positive side, it means the confessing of our faith in God's Word. Jesus declared in Matthew 10:32 (KJV), "Whosoever therefore shall confess me before men, him will I confess also before my Father which is in heaven." Psalms 116:10 (KJV) reminds us, "I believed, therefore have I spoken." In 2 Corinthians 4:13 (KJV) the Apostle Paul says, "We having the same spirit of faith, according as it is written, I believed and therefore have I spoken; we also believe, and therefore speak."

Question: Can you use you mouth to effectuate power?

Confession is saying the same thing with our mouth that God says in His Word. It is literally making the words of our mouth agree with the written Word of God.

If faith is going to move in our lives, it must have a means of expressing itself. The words of our lips give expression and life to the action of faith within us. Faith that does not speak is stillborn (dead). Romans 10: 8-10 (KJV) teaches on the subject of confession. Consider the relationship between the heart and the mouth, "But what saith it? The word is nigh thee, even in thy mouth, and in thy heart: that is, the word of faith, which we preach; That if thou shalt confess with thy mouth the Lord Jesus, and shalt believe in thine heart that God hath raised him from the dead, thou shalt be saved. For with the heart man believeth unto righteousness; and with the mouth confession is made unto salvation.

In verse 8, Paul mentions the mouth first, and the heart second. In verse 9, it is the mouth first and the heart second. But in verse 10, the order is reversed and the heart is mentioned first and the mouth second. This illustrates an important scriptural principle. The true power in Christ is disseminated according to what we think, and then say. With a conviction of what is on the inside, we can speak to the issues of life with authority. We can speak to illness, bringing the Word of God against the sickness. We can speak to poverty, bringing the Word of God against poverty. We can speak against strongholds; bring the Word of God against them. According to the pattern of these scriptures, it is necessary for us to begin by putting God's word in our mouth as an act of our will, and bring it against our problems. By confessing, or saying the same thing with our mouth as what God says in His Word, we receive it into our heart. The more often we confess with our mouth, the more firmly it becomes established in our heart.

Just a thought: There are some rules for usage of the mouth!

There are two reciprocal laws operating in the spiritual realm: The law of the Spirit Life in Christ Jesus and the law of sin and death. Faith energizes and activates the law of spirit life while fear, doubt and reaction activates the law of sin and death, both are initiated by the tongue. You employ one or the other by what your mouth and tongue releases. By speaking God's words into a situation you release the authority of spirit life. By speaking man's words into a situation you release the authority of sin and death, which is failure. By the power of the establishing witness, "spirit life" is spoken and validated. Consider the following evidence: Matthew 18: 16 (KJV), "But if he will not hear thee, then take with thee one or two more, that in the mouth of two or three witnesses every word may be established." Deuteronomy 19:15 (KJV) teaches us, "One witness shall not rise up against a man for any iniquity, or for any sin, in any sin that he sinneth: at the mouth of two witnesses, or at the mouth of three witnesses, shall the matter be established." Hebrews 10:28 (KJV) states, "He that despised Moses' law died without mercy under two or three witnesses." 1 Timothy 5:19 (KJV) states, "Against an elder receive not an accusation, but before two or three witnesses."

Question: Do you know that your eyes can lie to you?

To break free of a pattern of failure you must stop mindlessly validating whatever your physical senses perceive. What you see, hear, and feel is transitory. It is subject to change. The Word of God is true, unchanging, and eternal. We must choose to endorse our blessings through an understanding of establishment. We must learn that the power given to men on earth is a power that is spoken. What you think does not matter as much as what you say with your mouth. What you see is not necessarily true. How you react to situations usually dictates what you say, and then what you say dictates the outcome. Therefore we must examine how you react to things. There are three levels of reaction: the level of reason, the level of good conduct and the level of God's Spirit Life (transcendent). The person that lives on the level of reason will react temperamentally and emotionally. The person that lives on the level of good conduct will react patiently. But the person that lives on the level of God's Spirit Life will react transcendently.

Here's a puzzle: One plus one may not equal two!

We were taught multiplication tables in elementary school. We were taught by repetition. The more we repeated the tables, the more we believed. That is why today you know that 9 times 5 equal 45. When I ask you what is 9 times 5 you are not doing the math, you are calling to remembrance that which you repeated to yourself. You believe that 9 times 5 equal 45. My oldest son graduated from an Ivy League school, minoring in math. He would tell you that according to theory, no value maintains its value for any given period of time. In quantum theory math, an obvious answer is not necessarily the answer, therefore, what appears to be correct is not always correct. If you have 9 cases of open soda pop with 5 bottles per case, it would appear that you would have 45 bottles of soda pop. However, if evaporation diminishes the content of the bottles, you would have to establish the proper equation to justify content versus container. The content must be correctly established to consider worth. Therefore, your 9 cases with 5 bottles in each case may actually be a total of 44.5 bottles according to content. Instead of focusing on how much or how many, focus on the content. It is what's in the bottles that establish the value, not the bottle itself. An empty bottle is just an empty bottle. An empty vessel is just an empty vessel. You see, this is why some people cannot seem to be blessed. They are always counting the bottles and never establishing content. Here is how you deal with content instead of empty bottles. Whenever you are attacked by the enemy, you come to God's Word and begin immediately confess it openly with your mouth. The struggle ensues. The Word of God is saying something contrary to what you are experiencing. You must resist your feelings and make the words of your mouth agree with God's Word.

Practice your *homologeo* (confession). Keep saying it until you release your faith. Once you release your faith the struggle will be over and then it will become a natural process for you to speak with your mouth what God says in His Word. Confession, with the mouth, is the doorway of faith. It unlocks the wealth of God's promises on our behalf. This is the incredible truth that every believer must get hold of. We take hold of God's provision for us in every arena of our life by entering into a confession.

The power is in what we speak and say. The sacrifice of praise should be the act of confessing. Praising the Lord, will lead you into a total manifestation of God's Providence. Praise is confession and confession to God is praise. When two or three of us come together and enter into the presence of God through our praise, our spirits are released to believe God for miracles. When the entire congregation comes together corporately and enters into the sacrifice of praise and confession, there is a massive faith release that ushers in miracles. This corporate and massive praise and confession moves against the power of strongholds that bind the minds and bodies of the saints. Now, all things are possible.

Reflection: Power to live comes when we train our mouths to parallel God's Word. Try it!

PowerPoints!

- **Release your prayer language.**
- **Stop speaking counterproductive language.**
- **Speak what you mean and mean what you say.**
- **In your prayers, return God's Word back to Him.**
- **Your heart is deceitful, control it.**
- **When you do not know what to say, praise God.**
- **When you do know what to say, say it and then praise God.**
- **Make your words parallel God's Holy Word.**

CHAPTER SIX

THE POWER OF THE HOLY GHOST

Power for living only comes through the Holy Ghost; no presence, no power. He is the source of all power. Jesus told the apostles that they would have to wait for a power that would come from on high. The Lord Jesus Christ taught us in John 16:13 (KJV), "Howbeit when he, the Spirit of truth, is come, he will guide you into all truth: for he shall not speak of himself; but whatsoever he shall hear, that shall he speak: and he will shew you things to come." Our relationship with God depends totally on what God has done through Jesus Christ, so the power to live comes totally from God. To live the life as God intends, we must continually draw upon God's power, through the Holy Spirit.

The Greek word for the Holy Ghost is, *parakletos*, meaning one called alongside to help, to defend as an attorney. Now I know he's my personal spiritual lawyer and advocate because 1 John 2:1 (KJV) tells me, "My little children, these things write I unto you, that ye sin not. And if any man sin, we have an advocate with the Father, Jesus Christ the righteous." While some will look for F. Lee Bailey and Johnnie Cochran I'll settle for the Holy Ghost. He is the entire advocate I need. The simple truth is that we can only be strong, productive and prosperous through the work of the Holy Ghost in us. It is the Holy Ghost that assures us that we are the children of God. "The Spirit itself beareth witness with our spirit, that we are the children of God." (Romans 8:16, KJV) The only power we can have to effectuate authority in the earth comes with the Holy Ghost. Acts 1:8 (KJV) declares, "But ye shall receive power, after that the Holy Ghost is come upon you: and ye shall be witnesses unto me both in Jerusalem, and in all Judaea, and in Samaria, and unto the uttermost part of the earth."

It is the Holy Ghost in us that prays for our healing, "Likewise the Spirit also helpeth our infirmities: for we know not what we should pray for as we ought: but the Spirit itself maketh intercession for us with groanings which cannot be uttered." (Romans 8:26, KJV) You must believe in the ministry of the Holy Ghost in your life so that you can carry out the will of God for your life. The Holy Ghost never leaves you alone during the storms of life or when you go through a valley, drought or a trial. Any suffering that you endure is only temporary because the Holy Ghost is there ministering to your needs. The Holy Ghost does not come and go based upon the circumstances of your life. He is there when things are going well and He is there when things are bad.

Question: Since you believed, have you received the Holy Ghost?

You may not perceive yourself to be evangelical or Pentecostal and may shy away from this premise, but I say to you, without the Holy Ghost there is no power. Christianity, without the indwelling of the Holy Spirit is only religion. Our belief must go beyond religion and move into the realm of the spirit. God is a spirit and they that worship Him must worship Him in spirit and truth.

Just a thought: This is where I lose some of you!

Now there is a broader understanding that we must thrash out to fully enjoy the benefits of the Holy Ghost. Scripture teaches us that receiving the Holy Ghost at salvation is not the same as being filled with the Holy Ghost. I know I'm right because the apostles followed Jesus for three years and only later were filled with the Holy Ghost on the Day of Pentecost. Now the evidence of that indwelling was other tongues as the Spirit gave them utterance. God's Word shows that a person receives the indwelling of the Holy Ghost as a mark or identity, confirming that he or she really is a child of God. Jesus answered Nicodemus in the third chapter of the Gospel of John in the fifth and sixth verses, "Verily, verily, I say unto thee, Except a man be born of water and of the Spirit, he cannot enter into the kingdom of God. That which is born of the flesh is flesh; and that which is born of the Spirit is spirit." Romans 8:9 (KJV) states, "But ye are not in the flesh, but in the Spirit, if so be that the Spirit of God dwell in you. Now if any man have not the Spirit of Christ, he is none of his." Galatians 4:6 (KJV) states, "And because ye are sons, God hath sent forth the Spirit of his Son into your hearts, crying, Abba, Father." You can be saved but not necessarily filled or baptized with the Holy Ghost. We receive the Holy Ghost as a mark of identity.

"A walk in the Spirit will of necessity be a walk in accordance with the Word the Spirit has inspired. The parallel between Ephesians 5:18-21 and Colossians 3:15-17 is significant. The same results are said to flow from being filled with the Spirit in the first cast, and being filled with the Word in the second. To remain filled with the Spirit, and thus enjoy His continuing sanctifying work, will mean continuing to be filled with the Word. The relationship is obvious." *J.O. Sanders, Enjoying Intimacy with God, Moody, p. 91.*

Another thought: Here is where I get you back.

Charles Finney wrote how God gave him mighty infillings of the Holy Spirit: "I immediately found myself endued with such power from on high that a few words dropped here and there to individuals were the means of their immediate conversion. My words seemed to fasten like barbed arrows in the souls of men. They cut like a sword. They broke the heart like a hammer. Multitudes can attest to this. Sometimes I would find myself in a great measure empty of this power. I would go and visit, and find that I made no saving impression. I would exhort and pray with the same results. I would then set apart a day for private fasting and prayer…after humbling myself and crying out for help, the power would return upon me with all its freshness. This has been the experience of my life." *Touch the World Through Prayer, W. Duewel, OMS, p. 232*

Consider Acts 19: 1 – 6 (KJV), "And it came to pass, that, while Apollos was at Corinth, Paul having passed through the upper coasts came to Ephesus: and finding certain disciples, He said unto them, Have ye received the Holy Ghost since ye believed? And they said unto him, we have not so much as heard whether there be any Holy Ghost. And he said unto them, unto what then were ye baptized? And they said unto John's baptism. Then said Paul, John verily baptized with the baptism of repentance, saying unto the people, that they should believe on him which should come after him, that is, on Christ Jesus. When they heard this, they were baptized in the name of the Lord Jesus. And when Paul had laid his hands upon them, the Holy Ghost came on them; and they spake with tongues, and prophesied." The Apostle Paul commanded the Ephesians believers to "be filled with the Spirit." Salvation is the beginning of God's work in you. We now strive for the "perfecting."

The "perfecting" is the enabling power of God in the earth. It only comes with the indwelling of God's Holy Spirit in you. Paul instructed the saints to be not drunk with wine, but be ye filled with the spirit. As it is with our salvation versus the reception of God's Holy Spirit within us, so it was that Passover must precede Pentecost. Passover was the celebration of God's salvation for the Israelite children, when the angel of death passed over their homes taking the elder sons of all others. The Passover represents a "salvation." God spared and saved you. But Pentecost represents the power of God given in you. The time lapse between Passover and Pentecost is 50 days. In that time frame we see Peter and the other disciples saved but not filled. The filling came at Pentecost. Salvation was already given, but power was given on the Day of Pentecost.

The Pentecostal experience enables believers to receive power to gather their harvest. There are some denominations that erroneously teach that people are not saved until they receive the Holy Ghost and speak with tongues. This is not correct. They are saved, but not empowered. We must first have an experience with Jesus, allowing His blood to cleanse us from sin; then we become candidates for the baptism of the Holy Ghost.

Question: Can you deny the work and authority of the Holy Spirit?

Gregory of Nazianzus wrote, "The deity of the Holy Spirit ought to be clearly recognized in Scripture. Look at these facts: Christ is born; the Spirit is His forerunner. Christ is baptized; the Spirit bears witness. Christ is tempted; the Spirit leads Him up. Christ ascends; the Spirit takes His place. What great things are there in the character of God which are not found in the Spirit? What titles which belong to God are not also applied to Him? He is called the Spirit of God, the Spirit of Christ, the mind of Christ, the Spirit of the Lord, the Spirit of adoption, of truth, of liberty; the Spirit of wisdom, of understanding, of counsel, of might, of knowledge, of godliness, of the fear of God. This only begins to show how unlimited He is."

Reflection: The greatest challenge for some is receiving the Holy Spirit. This is where traditional denominational concepts fly in the face of true bible understanding. Power for living can only be attained through the Holy Ghost. Salvation is easy, living is hard!

PowerPoints!

- **Without the Holy Ghost you're a Corvette with no engine.**
- **Without the Holy Ghost you're simply religious.**
- **With the Holy Ghost you are spiritually powerful.**
- **Release the power of the Spirit from within.**
- **The ability to overcome is given by God's Spirit.**
- **The ability to know and discern are gifts of His Spirit.**
- **Receive His Spirit, receive His power.**
- **Move in the power of His Spirit.**

CHAPTER SEVEN

THE POWER TO SEE IT, SAY IT, SEIZE IT!

Phillips Brooks wrote, "Sad is the day for any man when he becomes absolutely satisfied with the life that he is living, the thoughts he is thinking and the deeds he is doing; until there ceases to be forever beating at the door of his soul a desire to do something larger which he seeks and knows he was meant and intended to do."

Let's visit Isaiah and study chapter fifty-five, verses 10 – 13 (KJV), "For as the rain cometh down, and the snow from heaven, and returneth not thither, but watereth the earth, and maketh it bring forth and bud, that it may give seed to the sower, and bread to the eater: So shall my word be that goeth forth out of my mouth: it shall not return unto me void, but it shall accomplish that which I please, and it shall prosper in the thing whereto I sent it. For ye shall go out with joy, and be led forth with peace: the mountains and the hills shall break forth before you into singing, and all the trees of the field shall clap their hands. Instead of the thorn shall come up the fir tree, and instead of the brier shall come up the myrtle tree: and it shall be to the LORD for a name, for an everlasting sign that shall not be cut off."

There are three levels of living. First is the "see-it" level, which is the bottom level. Anybody and everybody can easily live at this level. Everyone has an opportunity to visibly see. But what I am actually discussing is seeing faith's opportunity!

Did you know: Some of us are visually acute, but blind to opportunity!

I was driving to Nashville for the meeting of the National Association of Religious Broadcasters. Riding with me were two members of my staff. One of my pastor's was following me in another car. Being raised a hunter my eyes are trained to see game. Along the way I spotted deer grazing in a field and pointed them out. Then I spotted deer along the highway grazing in the grass. My two staffers may have never spotted the deer, because their eyes are not trained to see them. Upon our arrival in Nashville I asked the pastor following us, "Did you see the deer by the roadside along the way? He replied, what deer? All those animals were in the range of my vision, because I have been trained to see them. The see-it level is faith's opportunity. Many of us can be looking in the same direction, but that does not mean that all of us will see the same thing.

The second level is the "say-it" level. The see-it is the opportunity for faith; to say it is the word of faith. This is where you have to verbally commit yourself to what is gripped in your vision. Now if you don't have any vision, you won't have anything to grip! Every believer must have some say-it faith. The bible is full of say-it faith. Consider what Paul says to the saints at Rome, "If you confess with your mouth Jesus is Lord, you shall be saved." Romans 10:9 (NLT). And Jesus said unto them, "Because of your unbelief: for verily I say unto you, If ye have faith as a grain of mustard seed, ye shall say unto this mountain, Remove hence to yonder place; and it shall remove; and nothing shall be impossible unto you." (Matthew 17:20, KJV) Word faith is the say-it level. By the power of God's Word we speak to the issues of life.

Just a note: Don't be alarmed by the word "seize." God often commands His people to seize what He has ordained for them!

Thirdly, we have the "seize-it" level of living. This is where faith becomes action. It is more than vision, and it is more than verbiage. It is a vital action based and predicated on see-it and say-it. Because of the authority of faith a person can act. Since everyone starts on level one, the see-it level, we all have the opportunity to grab hold of faith's opportunity.

But as you climb the holiness ladder, fewer and fewer people climb with you. When you get to the seize-it stage, the action stage, you will find yourself in an elite group; most people never climb this high. They miss faith's opportunity and life's action.

What we fail to remember is that Jesus wants us to be fruitful. The theme of John 15 is Jesus wants us to live fruitful lives. Look at John 15:16 (NIV), "You did not choose me, but I chose you, and appointed you, that you should go and bear fruit, and that your fruit should remain, that whatever you ask the Father in my name, He may give it to you." But to be able to live a fruitful life you must have the proper attitude to manifest blessings in your life. From the previous chapter, this comes through the presence of the Holy Ghost in your life.

Question: Are you waiting for the tide to come in?

In the days before modern harbors, a ship had to wait for the flood tide before it could make it to port. The term for this situation in Latin was *ob portu*, that is, a ship standing over off a port, waiting for the moment when it could ride the turn of the tide to harbor.

The English word opportunity is derived from this original meaning. The captain and the crew were ready and waiting for that one moment for they knew that if they missed it, they would have to wait for another tide to come in. Shakespeare turned this background of the exact meaning of opportunity into one of his most famous passages. It's from Julius Caesar, Act 4, Scene 3:

> *There is a tide in the affairs of men,*
> *Which, taken at the flood, leads on to fortune;*
> *Omitted, all the voyage of their life*
> *Is bound in shallows and in miseries.*
> *On such a full sea are we now afloat;*
> *And we must take the current when it serves,*
> *Or lose our ventures.*

My grandmother knew misery and became comfortable with it and proficient in it. Many saints are like that. A person can become so accustomed to trouble that struggle becomes normal and success becomes abnormal. Mary Adkins was also poor and proud of it. I remember one sweltering Mississippi summer, asking her if she would ask God for an air conditioner. She told me that if God wanted her to have an air conditioner He would give one to her. I replied, but how does He know you want one? She replied I don't want one. Unbelievable as it may seem, that blessed old woman would choose to suffer versus succeed. Somewhere in her theology was the old "don't ask for stuff syndrome." This powerful woman of God, like so many others, misconstrued mammon as always bad. I attempted to instruct her that mammon itself is not bad; worshipping it is! She could pray heaven down to earth. Angels had to stop what they were doing and listen to her. She was gifted to heal and many sought her counsel. Yet, she never utilized that spiritual muscle in a way to better her family's condition. Truly noble, but genuinely mislead by notions of "glorious poverty."

Just a note: When you don't have any money please realize that you are not poor, you only have a temporary cash flow problem!

There is still within much of the Christian community a "knee jerk" reaction to prosperity. This whole concept of "see it, say it, seize it" must be at the least, worrisome to some. They will quickly relegate this thesis to "pie in the sky" religion. But it is not! It is living in Christ, through the Holy Ghost in power, affirming God's Word in the earth. It is not Rolls Royce's, Bentley's and Mercedes, but it may be Chevy's, Ford's and Chrysler's. The quality by which a Christian lives is testimony of God in their lives. I am convinced that God blesses us not only for ourselves but for the eyes of unbelievers. Much of the fourth chapter of Philippians is about contentment. But Paul declares that he knows how to have and how to have not. Neither dominates. It is the duty of a true believer to step out in faith and live to the absolute best he or she can. The same Apostle wrote to Ephesus, "The eyes of your understanding being enlightened; that you may know what is the hope of His calling, what are the riches of the glory of His inheritance in the saints, and what is the exceeding greatness of His power toward us who believe, according to the working of His mighty power which He worked in Christ when He raised Him from the dead and seated Him at His right hand in the heavenly places, far above all principality and power and might and dominion, and every name that is named, not only in this age but also in that which is to come. And He put all things under His feet, and gave Him to be head over all things to the church, which is His body, the fullness of Him who fills all in all." Ephesians 1: 18 – 23 (NKJV)

Question: What bible are some of these people reading?

Power to live was given by the Lord Jesus to the church. He had the power and commitment to die, but gave us the power to live. If we do not believe in asking and receiving then we do not believe in His Word. The entire notion of living in lack is a conspiracy from hell itself. It is a curse. Satan uses our own theology to confuse us. To affirm God's Word to the masses takes more than spoken words, it takes living examples. Living epistles must represent the Kingdom of God with the authority that He gave us. In a sermon I once discussed Christians that constantly complain. You know the type. Just ask them how they're doing and this is what you get, "Oh I could be better if my blood pressure were lower." Or, "You know my husband was laid off, the car is broken down and I need an operation." In the midst of that sermon I promptly requested that those people refrain from offering testimony to anyone at anytime. I'm also reminded of a young man that approached me in a supermarket and asked if he could come to my church and conduct a financial seminar. Upon quick examination, not judgment, I noticed that his shoes were worn and his suit was frail. I asked him, "How well are you doing financially?" He replied, "Not well at all, that is why I need to do some seminars." I really wanted to take the time and give him a bible lesson, but instead I prayed for his prosperity. He had the zeal, but no knowledge.

See it, say it and seize it are simple guidelines for those that truly believe. These are fundamentals that are found from the Garden of Eden to the Promised Land and from Bethlehem to Calvary. It is not taking, it is having. Power to live is available to those who stand on God's promises.

Dr. Bill Bright of Campus Crusade for Christ tells this story of a famous oil field called Yates Pool: During the depression this field was a sheep ranch owned by a man named Yates. Mr. Yates wasn't able to make enough on his ranching operation to pay the principal and interest on the mortgage, so he was in danger of losing his ranch.

With little money for clothes or food, his family (like many others) had to live on government subsidy. Day after day, as he grazed his sheep over those rolling West Texas hills, he was no doubt greatly troubled about how he would pay his bills. Then a seismographic crew from an oil company came into the area and told him there might be oil on his land. They asked permission to drill a wildcat well, and he signed a lease contract. At 1,115 feet they struck a huge oil reserve. The first well came in at 80,000 barrels a day. Many subsequent wells were more than twice as large. In fact, 30 years after the discovery, a government test of one of the wells showed it still had the potential flow of 125,000 barrels of oil a day. And Mr. Yates owned it all. The day he purchased the land he had received the oil and mineral rights. Yet, he'd been living on relief. A multimillionaire living in poverty, he didn't know the oil was there even though he owned it. Many Christians live in spiritual poverty. They are entitled to the gifts of the Holy Spirit and his energizing power, but they are not aware of their birthright.

Reflections: God's love for us goes directly to the temporal as well as the spiritual. He is concerned about the quality of our living. Jesus declared in John 10:10 the purpose of the thief, but He also declared His purpose, "That they might have life and have it more abundantly." Every Christian should strive for excellence in all areas of endeavor!

PowerPoints!

- **The devil is a liar. You can prosper and be in the Lord.**
- **Bind up satanic harassment and release heavenly empowerment.**
- **Do not become comfortable with mediocrity.**
- **Say to yourself daily, "I can do better."**
- **Proclaim your worthiness to be blessed.**
- **Establish the goals, say them to God, and receive them.**

CHAPTER EIGHT

POWER TO RECLAIM THAT WHICH WAS LOST

I was listening to the radio when I came across a country station and heard this fellow singing, "Enough is enough, and I'm taking back my stuff." It seems this fellow was upset that the person he loved apparently betrayed him and now he wants his gifts back. He proclaims, "Enough is enough." I thought about some of the darker events of my life, distressed times, painful situations, lost hope, unfulfilled dreams, betrayals, and missed opportunities and I came to the realization that Satan was the author of all that misery.

If you examine your life you will see that Satan has robbed you from time to time:

- He has taken your joy.
- He stole your good health.
- He disrupted your happy home.
- He manifested himself in your family members.
- He attacked your children.
- He put people in your life to hinder you.
- He engineered accidents.
- He messed up your finances.
- He stole your peace and substituted stress.
- He took your good mental health and gave you low self-esteem and depression.
- He stole your hope and left you hopeless.

Through the lack of spiritual stamina Satan waits until we are weak and then attacks. Like a predator on the plains of Africa, he seeks the weakest link. He waits until you are wounded or tired and attacks, robbing you of all that God has intended for you. Stealing your dreams and giving you nightmares. But if we live in faith and obedience we won't have anything to fear. He may harass and attack, worry and deceive, confuse and tempt, but the Word of God says, "For the weapons of our warfare are not carnal but mighty in God for pulling down strongholds." 2 Corinthians 10:4 (KJV)

Question: Are you willing to fight the very forces of evil?

But it goes further, Paul writes to Corinth in that sixth verse, "And being ready to punish all disobedience when your obedience is fulfilled." This means if we are obedient and faithful to God, the Lord gives us power to reclaim what we lost. The scripture says if we have a readiness, we can move on our on obedience and pull Satan down. Paul writes to Corinth in chapter 4 and verses 8 – 10 of this second letter, "We are troubled on every side, yet not distressed: we are perplexed, but not in despair; persecuted, but not forsaken; cast down, but not destroyed; always bearing about in the body the dying of the Lord Jesus." What this means is you can knock me down, but you can't knock me out. The boulders I stumble over are just pebbles. The logs that trip me up are just twigs.

The eagles that perturb me are just mosquitoes. The clod of dirt I worry about is just a speck of dust.

The Lord has given all of us spiritual authority over evil. We do not fight evil with evil, utilizing carnal weapons. With the weapons of our mind and physical might we will always lose. But when we use the weapons of faith we cannot be defeated. Jesus said to us in Matthew 16:19 (NLT) that He has given us the keys to the kingdom of heaven and we can decide what we will tolerate and what we will not tolerate. "And I will give you the keys of the kingdom of heaven, and whatsoever you bind on earth shall be bound in heaven and whatsoever you loose on earth shall be loosed in heaven." The newest and most correct translation of this scripture reads, "I will give you the keys of the kingdom of heaven, and whatever you forbid on earth must be what is already forbidden in heaven, and whatever you permit on earth must be what is already permitted in heaven."

This means that an obedient servant of God acts in concert with heaven, initiating the command on earth with heaven already in full accord. The Lord gives us the authority to forbid evil. In Matthew 18:18 the New Living Translation repeats itself with even more clarity, "I solemnly say to you, whatever you forbid on earth must be already forbidden in heaven, and whatever you permit on earth must be already permitted in heaven.

Just a note: Obedience unlocks the door of faith.

The key to this spiritual concert of action is obedience, seeking God's will before exercising spiritual authority in Jesus' name. The power of God only comes when we act according to His will. We must learn to minister in power. Jesus said in Matthew 12:28 (NASB), "But if I cast out demons by the Spirit of God, surely the kingdom of God has come upon you." The prophet Elisha was once faced with a mounting situation. The children of Israel were prepared to cross the Jordan and the King of Syria threatened them and one young man cried out, "What shall we do?" and Elisha answered, "Do not fear, for those who are with us are more than those who are with them." Elisha prayed to God for blindness upon his enemy and the army of Syria was struck blind. The apostle Paul would later characterize this by saying, "If God be for us, who can be against us." The Lord wants us to exercise our faith and spiritual authority over the presence of evil. He wants us to turn our walls into bridges. It is imperative all of us today dedicate and consecrate ourselves to the following:

We will bind up and heal old wounds.
We will heal our broken heart.
We will renew and restore our hope.
We will take back the joy that we once had.
We will retrieve the peace of happier times.
We will reconstruct happiness in our homes.
We will regain our optimism for brighter days.
We will prosper and refuse to be poor.
We will be in good health.

Just a thought: We need to stop allowing the enemy entrees into our lives. He is stoppable!

Here is a theological quagmire, "Christians ought to be willing to fight." The very essence of our faith teaches peace and humility. Yet, there is a need for a Christian to fight. There is a time for warfare and it is now. Satan is busier than ever, robbing people of everything God intends for them. John 10:10 declares that he (Satan) is a thief. My friend and hunting buddy is Judge Joe Brown from TV fame. Joe gained national attention as a criminal court judge here in Memphis when he ruled that a victim of a theft would be given the opportunity to go into the home of the thief and take whatever he chose of value to compensate him for his loss. I really liked that sentence. The whole notion of taking back what was stolen is appealing. This may appear as fighting evil with an evil but in actuality it is not. It is the act of reclamation. Reclaiming what was yours.

We have allowed the enemy to establish residence in our homes, offices and churches. He uses our doctrine against us to protect himself from attack. He reminds us that we are Christians and we should always forgive. He recites the beatitudes and ushers in a tolerant spirit. Enough is enough. Let's not be confused. Satan is to be treaded upon and not to be treated lightly. He is to be rebuked and never tolerated. We must command him to get behind us and put him in his proper place.

You will never develop power to live if you are not willing to fight for what you believe. Naïveté is unacceptable and complacency is intolerable. We are spiritual warriors fighting a spiritual battle. The enemy must be defeated and we must regain our position and place in God's favor. God is calling new legions of prayer warriors to attack and destroy the forces of evil in the earth. The believer of the 21st Century must be willing to meet, head-on, the opposing activities of the enemy with the uncompromising power of God.

Question: How about showing up and showing out!

There are three scriptures that I want to reference the King James Version of; Luke 18:1, 2 Corinthians 2:11, 1 Timothy 6:12. Luke writes, "And he spake a parable unto them to this end, that men ought always to pray, and not to faint." Paul writes to Corinth in his second letter, "Lest Satan should get an advantage of us: for we are not ignorant of his devices."

He writes to Timothy, "Fight the good fight of faith." The Bible states that believers should pray, and not faint lest Satan should get the advantage of us; for we are not ignorant of his devices. Jesus taught us in John 10:10 that the primary objective of Satan is to rob us, kill us (spiritually) and destroy every good thing God intends for us to have.

The enemy is plotting and planning your demise. Do you know his devices? The enemy is planning a shipwreck for your finances. Do you know his devices? The enemy is subverting the minds of your children. Do you know his devices? The enemy is planning a train wreck for your relationships. Do you know his devices? To reclaim what is rightfully yours the believer must understand that we are under attack.

The child of God in the 21st Century can not afford the luxury of benign neglect and indifference. We are called to a battle that must be fought. You cannot sit idly by while the enemy encamps all around the people you love. Paul writes to Timothy in his first letter and first chapter, verses 18, 19, "This charge I commit unto thee, son Timothy, according to the prophecies which went before on thee, that thou by them mightest war a good warfare; Holding faith, and a good conscience; which some having put away concerning faith have made shipwreck." (1Timothy 1:18-19 KJV) Every true believer must prepare to effectively utilize the Word of God to go into spiritual battle with an enemy that is hell bent on our demise. God is waiting on his spiritual warriors to show-up and show-out.

The Bible is a conglomerate of prophecies and promises that are to be used as weapons against the enemy. But first we must understand that we cannot fight with carnal skills. Worldliness will neutralize any ability you might have to fight off evil.

Too many people think that worldliness is something limited to external behavior. Other think worldliness is hanging out with the wrong kinds of people. Worldliness is a wrong attitude of the heart that indicates a lack of a totally consuming love for the Lord God. It is important to remember that the Lord hates sin. God's wrath is directed toward all forms of the sins of worldliness. Those who fail to commit themselves to the Lord Jesus will not only miss God's blessings but experience God's displeasure.

There are two divisions in the body today, the separatist and the condonist. The separatist believe that those who love the Lord must separate themselves from any and all things that are secular. The condonist conform, or condone, to things of the world; political correctness and social behavior. The Lord desires neither of the two. What the Lord is looking for is the Transformist. This is the person that can live in the world, not tolerate it nor condone it but overcome it. Allow me to give this example; Jesus was with the prostitute, but was not w i t h the prostitute. Romans 12:2 (KJV) explains, "And be not conformed to this world: but be ye transformed by the renewing of your mind, that ye may prove what is that good, and acceptable, and perfect, will of God." God is releasing in us this day, in our lives the power to counteract every attack of Satan. God wants His people to gain jurisdictional authority over the powers of darkness by superimposing the plans and purposes of God over the plans and purposes of the enemy. It's time to show-up and show-out, reclaiming things that are lost.

Here's a thought: It walks like a duck, quacks like a duck, but is it really a duck?

Do not be in love with the world, live in it, overcome it, but don't be of it. "Stop loving this evil world and all that it offers you, for when you love the world, you show that you do not have the love of the Father in you. For the world offers only the lust for physical pleasure, the lust for everything we see and the pride of our possessions. These are not from the Father. They are from this evil world." (1 John 2:15, 16, KJV) Jesus teaches us in John 16:33 (KJV), "These things I have spoken unto you, that in me ye might have peace. In the world ye shall have tribulation: but be of good cheer; I have overcome the world."

The believer must have overcoming power and authority. To reclaim that which is lost we must overrule every diabolical sanction, subverting activity, injunction, directive, mandate or order, which opposes the will of God concerning our lives and our families. We must overthrow, overtake all demonic undertakings, internal and external. We must resist satanic contentions, intentions, provocations and negotiations concerning the lives of the ones we love. We must strike at the very heart of evil alliances against us.

David is going to help us now. You see David understood not to pray his problem, but to pray his power. "Then David said to the Philistine, "You come to me with a sword, with a spear, and with a javelin. But I come to you in the name of the LORD of hosts, the God of the armies of Israel, whom you have defied. This day the LORD will deliver you into my hand ... that all the earth may know that there is a God in Israel. And everyone assembled here will know that the LORD rescues his people, but not with sword and spear. This is the LORD's battle, and he will give you to us." (1 Samuel 17:45-47, NLT) Saul and Israel were allowing the Philistines to define them. David chose not to be a separatist or conformist and allow sin and the way of the world to define him. A true believer must define his or herself through their faith. David wrote in Psalms 144:1 (KJV), "Blessed be the LORD my strength, which teaches my hands to war, and my fingers to fight."

The enemy is so sophisticated that he uses our Bible against us. Many won't fight because they read "blessed are the peacemakers." Some won't fight because they see that the "meek shall inherit the earth." Some won't fight because they read that the Lord will fight our battles for us. All of the above is true, but taken out of context and exegeted improperly. The 21st Century Christian must become aware that the Word of God teaches kingdom authority. This authority must be employed for the reclamation of the lost.

Reflections: A guy was using dynamite to fish. He would throw in a stick, it would explode and fish would float up to the surface. His friend in the boat with him said, "You can't do that, it's illegal." The fellow lit the fuse of another stick of dynamite and gave it to his friend and asked, "Are you going to talk or fish?" Sometimes we are pushed beyond our rationale in dealing with a situation. Satan is merciless and does not deserve any compassion. Fish!

PowerPoints!

- Aren't you tired of being victimized by evil? Stop it now!
- Remember your joy of yesteryear and reclaim it.
- Every prophet of God had to face an enemy, so do you.
- Tell yourself, "I'm better than that."
- Reclaim your home for God.
- Declare your job as being under your authority.
- Remember, weapons may form, but they won't prosper against you.
- Turn walls into bridges.

CHAPTER NINE

KARATE POWER FOR THE SOUL

The writer of Hebrews instructed us, "Wherefore seeing we also are compassed about with so great a cloud of witnesses, let us lay aside every weight, and the sin which doth so easily beset us, and let us run with patience the race that is set before us, Looking unto Jesus the author and finisher of our faith; who for the joy that was set before him endured the cross, despising the shame, and is set down at the right hand of the throne of God." (Hebrews 12:1, 2, KJV)

Why is it that some of us set goals only to fail and never reach them? Why does success elude some people who truly want to be successful? The problem is not external, material, or circumstantial. Again, the problem is spiritual. Winning takes effort. Surviving only requires attendance, being alive. Winning through Christ is faith walking. Surviving is existing, living under the tyranny of circumstance and situation. The word here says there is a race before us. We run races to win, not just to participate. Jesus is the author and finisher of our faith. It is in Him that we believe. Without faith it is impossible to please Him.

Why don't some Christians win?

1. The totality of their relationship with God is only in worship attendance.
2. They have not developed a praying spirit.
3. They don't witness because they are ashamed in the presence of others.

4. They are sight walkers and therefore only believe and hope for what they can see.

Here's a thought: We must fight for that which is right.

The martial arts give instruction in bodily self defense. Karate is one of those defense systems. Pupils of Karate are taught that real power comes from true belief. A person must believe they are capable of defending themselves. Christians should think likewise. We must believe that we can win in all situations. If you only see your physical size versus the larger size of an opponent you will quickly deduce that you cannot win. However karate teaches that size doesn't matter. Your ability is directly attributed to your training, not your size. Therefore you cannot believe your eyes and what they may deduce. Seeing is not always believing but rather believing is seeing. Romans 8:24 (KJV) teaches, "For we are saved by hope: but hope that is seen is not hope: for what a man seeth, why doth he yet hope for?"

A true believer must live the exemplary life of a believer. This means we must accomplish goals and achieve in spite of current circumstance and condition. Paul wrote to the Philippians 4: 12, 13 (KJV), "I know both how to be abased, and I know how to abound: every where and in all things I am instructed both to be full and to be hungry, both to abound and to suffer need. I can do all things through Christ which strengtheneth me." Paul writes that I am instructed both to be full and to be hungry, both to abound and to suffer need. The writer of Hebrews says we are surrounded by a host of encouragers (witnesses), both those who are living and those who have gone on to be with the Lord. At the same time we must realize that there are also discouragers around us. They hinder our efforts and throw obstacles in our paths. The good news is that "we do not struggle alone." In addition we are not the first to struggle spiritually. Others before us have run this race and won. Their witness is with us. Paul wrote to the Ephesians in 6:12 (KJV), "For we wrestle not against flesh and blood, but against principalities, against powers, against the rulers of the darkness of this world, against spiritual wickedness in high places." The *"Adkinsnazation"* of this scripture is as follows: "For we are not fighting other people, so let us stop focusing on other people, but it is evil in other people, the ruler of this world that seeks our destruction.

Therefore we need to be skilled and prepared to fight for, and to defend God's intended blessings for us." We live with and face daily demons under the control of Satan that desire to defeat us. Although the Word of God assures us victory, we must engage in the struggle until the Lord returns. The problem for some of you is that you are not engaged in the struggle. To be in a struggle is to know that you are in a fight.

David understood struggle and dealing with demons. David was a man who came to knowledge of the Lord as a youngster. He was anointed by God to meet a giant in the Valley of the Shadow of Death. And even David's defeat of Goliath did not mean that his life would be a bed of roses after that. David endured hardship after hardship, and a jealous King that wanted him dead. These situations, however, were ones that strengthened David and further prepared him for greater things ahead. David was not defeated by jealousy, exile, warring enemies, traitorous followers, rebellious children, or even his own sinfulness. He was not defeated because in each instance, David turned to the Lord in repentance and in trust. Some Christians don't win because they turn inward to self instead of turning back to God.

Question: Do you have winning ways?

Look at the Apostle Peter. Peter certainly had failures and made mistakes. He rebuked Jesus when Jesus spoke of His crucifixion. He failed in his faith when it came to calming a storm. He relied on his own strength when he cut off the ear of a high priest's servant, and he denied Jesus three times after His arrest. The Lord still found favor upon Peter and he discipled thousands of believers into the faith. Peter understood that winning for Christ was his mandate. In spite of his own short-comings the Lord could still use him. You will never realize your potential in Christ or the power of possibility in your life until you understand that winning and winning ways are necessary for every believer. David and Peter clearly understood this. Therefore winning takes effort and "rebound ability." Some of you cannot win because you have no rebound ability. Once you're down, you're down! But the Word of God says we must be prepared to not only rebound but to do battle. Hebrews 6:13 (KJV) says, "Wherefore take unto you the whole armor of God, that ye may be able to withstand in the evil day, and having done all, to stand." Taking on the armor of God means that the Christian is prepared to go into spiritual battle with a spiritual enemy. But to do this you must first loose some weight. You cannot fight Satan carrying around a lot of dead weight.

The Lord will give you the strength to loose the weight that so easily besets you. Weights are those things that trouble you, weigh heavily on your mind, and cause you to be worried, frustrated, afraid and discouraged. Some of this weight is sin. It is the sin that is present so easily in your life. Sins entangle us and cause us to miss out on God's blessings and opportunities. And some of this weight is guilt, guilt and embarrassment from past experiences that you can't shake. And then some of this weight maybe another person, unsaved and corruptive to your relationship with God, but influencing your life.

All of these weights must be put down. No one else can strip these things from your life other than you. You must take charge and lay aside those dead things that hold you back from your pursuit of Godliness. You are the one that must choose to run with endurance the race the Lord has set before you. So we put on the armor of the Lord and do battle. Believers need a spiritual fighting lesson. I call it "Karate for the Soul."

Just a thought: Dress for the occasion!

Here is your armor. We fight Satan with the "Strong Belt of Truth." Satan fights with lies, and sometimes his lies sound like truth; but only believers have God's truth, which can defeat Satan's lies. We fight Satan with the "Breastplate of God's Approval." Satan often attacks our hearts, the seat of our emotions, self-worth, and trust. God's approval is the breastplate that protects our hearts. He approves of us because he loves us and sent his Son to die for us. We fight Satan with "Shoes, Ready to Spread the Good News."

Satan wants us to think that testifying is a worthless and hopeless task. But the "shoes" God gives us are the motivation to continue to proclaim the true peace, which is available in God, good news everyone needs to hear. We fight Satan with the "Shield of Faith."

What we see are Satan's attacks in the form of insults, lies, setbacks, and temptations. But the shield of faith protects us from Satan's flaming arrows. With holy eyes we can see beyond our circumstances and know that ultimate victory is ours. We fight Satan with the "Helmet of Salvation." Satan wants to make us doubt God, Jesus and our salvation. The helmet protects our minds from doubting God's saving work for us. We fight Satan with the "Sword, the Word of God." The sword is the only weapon of offense in this list of armor. There are times when we need to take the offensive against Satan. When we are tempted, we need to trust in the truth of God's Word.

"Karate" teaches discipline for the defeat of an adversary or foe. It utilizes the principle of positive resistance against a negative force. We too, as believers, use the positive against the negative. The Christian must assume the responsibility of waging the battle. Others cannot do it for you. Others can, for the most part, only support you in your effort. This spiritual fight is what frees the soul from the tyranny of sin and failure. There are three obstacles that the believer must be willing to attack:

1. Fear. Fear paralyzes us and makes us feel inadequate. There are some good fears that we all need in our daily lives. These fears are normal; like the fear of falling, the fear of fire, or the fear of crossing a busy street. But there are also unnatural fears that are spiritual in their roots. These fears side track us from our goals and dismiss God's visions. Faith is the opposite of fear. It is the ultimate solution for fear.

2. Nagging Doubt. Doubt is closely related to fear. When you doubt, you become unsteady, tentative, and wavering in your pursuit of a goal or a vision. You are not paralyzed as in fear, but you are stymied by indecision. People doubt because they lack understanding that God is with them always.

3. Excuse-itis. This is an infection of self-justification and excuses that takes root and rots away at a person's initiative. It is the "blame game." Blaming a person, condition or situation for the lack of his or her own inadequacy. It is how we make ourselves feel better after we've quit.

When God's glory is strongly upon you it will disarm the evil forces and powers that are attacking you. James writes in 4:7, 8 (KJV), "Submit yourselves therefore to God. Resist the devil, and he will flee from you.

Draw nigh to God, and he will draw nigh to you. Cleanse your hands, ye sinners; and purify your hearts, ye double minded." Fear, nagging doubt and excuses will negate your potential to wage the battle. They must be overcome.

Traditional thinking has been God fights our battles for us. This is true; He fights the ones we can't fight for ourselves. There are some hills for us to climb, some rivers for us to cross. A defense must be made within the ability of the believer. Jesus taught that we have the power to tread upon serpents. We are able in faith, to withstand the forces of evil and to take evil head-on.

Let us pray. Father I speak the Words of power and anointing. I declare your authority given to me. I bind up all evil harassment and rebuke evil concentrations. I announce to the prince of this world that your Spirit is upon me and I now overthrow the plans and schemes of evil that have sat themselves against me. I pull down all strongholds and cast out every imagination and resist any and all temptations. I stand in the confidence of your Holy Word and believe completely in my victory to come. In the name, and by the blood of Jesus, Amen.

Here is a thought: My old football coach, Waddell P. Porter would often say, "If you want the ball you've got to take it. If you want to keep it, you've got to fight for it."

PowerPoints!

- **Run your race to win, not participate!**
- **God cannot be pleased without your faithfulness.**
- **The size of the enemy or your problem does not matter.**
- **Stop being a cream-puff Christian. Take a stand!**
- **Never apologize for what you believe and know to be true.**
- **Stop making excuses.**
- **Don't be afraid or reluctant to step on some snakes.**
- **Seek power to discern evil representation around you.**

CHAPTER TEN

THE POWER OF MONEY

E very Christian must learn that money is a vehicle, not a tool. Money is a means by which God allows you to accomplish according to His Will and His purpose. The bible teaches us that the love of money is the root of all evil. Money, itself, is not inherently evil. It is our lust and love of it that corrupts the nature and leads to sin. Charles Stanley wrote, "The Bible has more verses devoted to finances and money, and our proper use of them, than to verses about heaven! God knew money was a practical matter that would require our attention on a daily basis. Money is a vital part of our lives." *Experiencing Success God's Way, p. 53, 54.* We need power to live and we sometimes need money to live in power (meaning authority). Talk about money seems almost heretical to some of the old guard in the church. The gospels reveal many good believers that had money. It was a necessity even for Christ when taxes were due. God sometimes directs a certain amount of wealth towards us for the benefits of others. God blesses us with prosperity for others, especially the unsaved, to see. God's children are not to be poor, desolate and displaced. Neither are they to be wallowing in opulence and affluence for vanity sake. God's people should live good; well with quality of living not quantity of possessions. Poverty is a curse and should be regarded as such. An old deacon once said to me, "Reverend, the bible says the poor will always be with us." I replied, "But you don't have to be one of them."

Question: How do we get financial blessings?

The problem with most people is that they look for money in all the wrong places. I'm a deer hunter. Suppose I decided to hunt deer in downtown Memphis, taking with me the right camouflage, gun and accessories needed for a good deer hunt. The problem is I'm hunting in an area that is non-productive. I must hunt deer where deer can be found. Although there are deer in Tennessee, Downtown Memphis is not the right environment for deer. I'm spinning my wheels hunting deer in the wrong environment. Good hunting is all about location, location, location. God operates in the environment of obedience and if you want to catch Him you must pursue Him in obedience. Obedience is the best place to hunt for financial blessings. Matthew Henry once said, "There is an inexhaustible fullness of grace and mercy in God, which the prayers of all the saints can never draw dry. Whatever we may ask, or think to ask, still God is still able to do more, abundantly more, exceedingly abundantly more. Open thy mouth ever so wide, still he hath wherewithal to fill it."

Ephesians 3:20 (KJV) reminds us, "Now unto him that is able to do exceeding abundantly above all that we ask or think, according to the power that worketh in us." I truly enjoy the NIV translation of that scripture, "Now to him who is able to do immeasurably more than all we ask or imagine, according to his power that is at work within us." Consider this, if we would be so bold to ask for or seriously think about what only we dare dream about, even that is far below what God can deliver. For the Bible says He just won't do a little bit better or even a whole lot better, but ABUNDANTLY better. In fact, the word exceeding implies that abundant is not even a word big enough in meaning to describe what He is able to do. Now remember, money is a vehicle, not a tool. Money is transportation to the place you're trying to get to. For all these poor-mouth preachers who delight in telling you that your reward will come in the hereafter, realize quickly that Jesus is clearly saying I want you to live an abundant life (John 10:10). This can be translated to a life that bears witness to "fullness, wellness and whole-being," again, not necessarily opulence and decadent wealth.

Prosperity is a God idea, not a man creation. Too many Christians debate within their mind if prosperity is allowable. The problem is not the place where prosperity can be found. The problem is preparing the people to prosper. The place to hunt for your prosperity is first within you. When the children of Israel got to the Jordan River, God stopped the manna from flowing. When God is ready for you to cross he'll sometimes change your diet, in other words your living style, your habits. A Christian is not supposed to live from miracle to miracle. At some point we are to move into wellness. God's people are supposed to live in the abundance and the overflow of God's goodness, His mercy, and His provision. It is God's desire for you to prosper. Psalm 35:27 (KJV) says, "Let the Lord be magnified." Magnified literally means to swell up. It is allowable for us swell up with God's goodness. David declared that God takes pleasure in our prosperity. John, chapter fifteen declares that God's disciples will be known by the fruit produced in their lives. The Apostle John prayed in 3 John 2 (KJV), "Beloved, I wish above all things that thou mayest prosper and be in health, even as thy soul prospereth.

Here's a thought: Living with supernatural finances.

Now John says, "As your soul prospers." To prosper in your soul you must be at the place where God can be found. That place is obedience. Therefore to have supernatural finances you must have a prosperous soul first. God is not confined to the box of our imagination. God operates in the supernatural. Jesus told the woman at the well, "God is a spirit and they that worship Him must worship Him in spirit and truth." You hunt deer in the woods and you hunt supernatural finances in the spirit realm. If you want money prosper your soul. Remember, worship is "worth-ship." The enemy would have you to believe that you are not worthy. Stop saying that, you are! You are worthy and deserving of any and all of God's blessings.

Let's consider worship a little further. The literal Greek translation for worship is *proskuneo*, a compound word. It comes from pros, towards, and *kuneo*, to kiss. It is an act of homage, reverence, and is usually translated worship. The act of worship is the act of intimacy. In this loving relationship God returns your love with blessings. We give Him our praises, He gives us blessings.

Question: How do you get wealth?

Now understand this, God gives your hands the power to get wealth. Deuteronomy 8:18 (KJV) declares, "But thou shalt remember the LORD thy God: for it is he that giveth thee power to get wealth, that he may establish his covenant which he sware unto thy fathers, as it is this day." True wealth is supernatural, not monetary. Money itself, can not guarantee wealth. Wealth is a state of condition. In supernatural finances, money is a vehicle, it is not the place we're trying to get to, it is the way we're trying to get there. With God, real wealth does not require money, only anointing. Money can take you so far, but anointing can deliver you to the highest places. If you covet and cherish money you will never discover God's manner of provision. This is why so many people have money but not wealth. And in this case wealth can be translated as happiness, joy, peace and contentment. What is the point of having a lot of money and can't even sleep well at night? Again, we must see our wealth in the correct environment. God uses the principle of planting and harvesting to convey the Kingdom Principle of Giving and Receiving. In the natural world, you only reap what you sow. In the supernatural world you reap even more than you can think. So if you are a planter, that means you plant seeds, expecting to harvest. The seed is the giving. The harvest is the reaping. A good seed determines a good harvest. A seed planted never leaves you. It just goes into your future. Therefore, you cannot sow, being mindful of today's situations and circumstances. You sow your seed realizing that the harvest comes in the future. A seed planted leaves and goes into your future. The natural realm cannot bind you. God promises to prosper you when you give. The whole Kingdom system operates by sowing and reaping.

God gave man three gifts in the Garden of Eden. He gave him dominion and He gave him authority. Then the bible says God gave man seed, two kinds of seed; his own seed which is the seed of life and the herb bearing seed, which is the seed of sustenance. One seed is given for propagation the other is given for provision. The place of obedience begins with the obedience of giving. The gift of obedience only comes with the anointing of trust. Sow what God gave you. Consider Paul's declaration to the Galatians in 6:7, "Be not deceived; God is not mocked: for whatsoever a man soweth, that shall he also reap." Living with supernatural finances means you're living with God-money, not man-money. God-money is money that God gave you to take you somewhere. It is your vehicle to take you to the place where God wants you to be. God-money is far more effective than man-money. God-money multiplies at rates no bank can compete, hundred fold, and thousand fold. God-money may appear to be little, but it can accomplish far more than a lot of man-money. God-money can stretch and buy more than it should, accomplish more than it ought. God-money may not even be in your possession, it just might be in the possession of your enemy, but it's still yours. God-money is so awesome that no matter where it is it will still be used to benefit you. God-money can also be invisible. You can't see it, cannot touch it, but it is still there. I know I'm right, because this invisible money sometimes pays bills and you don't know where it came from. It is so proficient that sometimes you think you're broke and stuff keeps coming your way. God-money is also a heavenly annuity. Some of your God-money is stored up for the future. Your seed planted today, might reap a harvest in 2020. God won't give it to you now because you don't need it now.

Another Question: What do you need to know?

You need to know that the only thing that separates you from wealth is you. Wealth is all around you. You may currently have wealth but cannot recognize it because it has been misused. For the believer, money transports you from one state to another. It is a vehicle that is usable, not desired. Place no great emphasis on money itself, but what it can accomplish. Use it properly and above all do not give it reverence. We are privileged by God to use money and possessions to bless other people. We ought to be funnels, pathways for God's blessings to flow through us to others. The pursuit of wealth should not be our main priority. Jesus only produced money when money itself was a necessity. His wealth was established in His authority. Our wealth is established in our authority as well. Jesus taught us in Matthew 6: 19 – 21 (KJV), "Lay not up for yourselves treasures upon earth, where moth and rust doth corrupt, and where thieves break through and steal: But lay up for yourselves treasures in heaven, where neither moth nor rust doth corrupt, and where thieves do not break through nor steal: For where your treasure is, there will your heart be also."

Here's a thought: Don't hoard money. Establish the flow!

Hoarding money is counterproductive. Giving generously is the key. To be blessed financially is to establish a flow. There is a Danish proverb that says, "The perpetual saver always lives in poverty." What good is money if it is not used? What good is it for a church to have millions of dollars in a bank but no outreach ministry? The "flow" is the channel of blessings. Once the flow is established the channel is clarified. You can see God pouring His blessings into your living. Why, because you have sought your finances for His purpose, not your own. I sometimes sit and daydream of what accomplishments I could make for the kingdom if I had just a little more money. I think about the various ministries, missionary outreach programs and even new amenities I could install in the facility if I had just a little more money. And here is the good news; I always get more money to manifest those dreams. I fight off any notion of self and what can be done for self with additional monies. I live well and am content with my living (another key). Money is a medium of exchange, a vehicle, that's all. The believer knows that it is intended be used for righteous purposes. It is a blessing and should be regarded as such. Good stewardship is demanded for establishment of the "flow."

Reflection: Billy Graham once said, "If a person gets his attitude toward money straightened out, then almost all other areas of his life will be straightened out."

PowerPoints!

- **Money is supposed to take you somewhere! Go.**
- **Don't ever say you're broke; you only have a temporary cash flow problem.**
- **Can you afford to tithe? You can't afford not to.**
- **Take it in; let it go, establish the flow!**
- **We are privileged by God and are blessed because of it.**
- **A substantial seed brings a substantial harvest.**

CHAPTER ELEVEN

POWER TO TRANQUILIZE A TROUBLED SEA

There was a storm on a Galilean sea one day, "And the same day, when the even was come, he saith unto them, Let us pass over unto the other side. And when they had sent away the multitude, they took him even as he was in the ship. And there were also with him other little ships. And there arose a great storm of wind, and the waves beat into the ship, so that it was now full. And he was in the hinder part of the ship, asleep on a pillow: and they awake him, and say unto him, Master, carest thou not that we perish?

And he arose, and rebuked the wind, and said unto the sea, Peace, be still. And the wind ceased, and there was a great calm. And he said unto them, Why are ye so fearful? how is it that ye have no faith?" Mark 4: 35 – 40; 5: 1 – 8 (KJV)

Question: Are you a cliffhanger?

The story is told of a man who fell off a cliff, but managed to grab a tree limb on the way down. The following conversation ensued: "Is anyone up there?" "I am here. I am the Lord. Do you believe me?" "Yes, Lord, I believe. I really believe, but I can't hang on much longer." "That's all right; if you really believe you have nothing to worry about. I will save you. Just let go of the branch." A moment of pause, then the man said: "Is anyone else up there?" When the going gets tough, faith is often not our first reaction. Fear and panic usually come much more naturally to us.

All day Jesus was pressured and preaching in the hot sun, so by nightfall He was probably exhausted and He did what He often did. He said, brothers let's leave this crowd so I can get some rest. Jesus, the Lord of the Sabbath, understood the value of resting. So Jesus climbed in the back of the boat and fell asleep. But during His sleep a terrible storm raged through the Sea of Galilee and caused the disciples to fear for their lives. If you've ever been out to sea or on a big lake when a furious storm hits, you know it's very scary. I grew up fishing on Sardis Reservoir in Northern Mississippi. I've been out in some horrible storms. I can tell you, when nature's wrath is unleashed in the power of wind and water together it can be a helpless feeling. I've fought waves and wind and felt useless as the waves were too high and came crashing over the bow of my boat leaving ankle deep water in the boat. My bilge pump attempted to remove the water, but it was too much. The more it pumped, the more came in, it was a loosing battle. I've even had to spend the night on shore, across the lake, waiting for the morning and my chance to cross back to boat camp and dock.

Here's a thought: Don't scare your own self to spiritual death.

The apostles were in that type of wicked storm. A fierce gale of wind was whipping through the deep ravines, pouring into the Sea of Galilee. Those strong winds were creating giant waves that were consistently crashing onto the boat. They were getting absolutely pounded by the sea and the wind, to the point that the boat was on the brink of sinking or coming apart. It was a life-threatening storm. Now, you must now take particular note. Jesus was sleep in the boat while the stormed raged. All this fear was within the apostles, but Jesus was asleep. Jesus calmness and sleep was teaching His disciples the importance of faith over fear.

In the storm we tend to panic. In the storm we loose our faith. In the storm we turn to the wrong folk. In the storm we loose our grip. In the storm our flesh dominates our spirit. At that moment, the humanity and flesh of the apostles cried out to Jesus, "Don't you care about us?" Panic and fear can often come more natural than faith. But the really good news is there is a way to cast out fear and panic, it's through faith in Christ.

If you want to tranquilize your troubles you must first learn to speak faith-filled words (refer back to chapter four). Let's study and see what Jesus had to say about faith-filled words. In Mark chapter 11, verses 1 – 4 (KJV), we read, "And Jesus entered into Jerusalem, and into the temple: and when he had looked round about upon all things, and now the eventide was come, he went out into Bethany with the twelve. And on the morrow, when they were come from Bethany, he was hungry: And seeing a fig tree afar off having leaves, he came, if haply he might find any thing thereon: and when he came to it, he found nothing but leaves; for the time of figs was not yet. And Jesus answered and said unto it, No man eat fruit of thee hereafter for ever, And his disciples heard it." Jesus went to the tree because it had leaves and seemed productive, but found no figs. Jesus declares no men eat fruit from this tree forever and He walked off. When they came back the next day, the disciples noticed that the tree was now dead.

Here's a radical thought: Don't cuss, curse!

The word curse is not the word cuss. Cuss meaning to utilize profanity. The disciples said that Jesus cursed the tree. Curse means that Jesus spoke in negativism to it. The bible says that Jesus put a curse on it. Jesus knew that there was power in His words.

The words of negativity can kill and the words of faith can fulfill. When he spoke to the fig tree, it withered and died. The apostles were awestruck by this act of speaking and killing. But Jesus teaches them the exact opposite usage of words. Now notice in verse 22 Jesus said, "Have faith in God." This actually translates, have the God kind of faith. In Romans 12:3 (KJV) the bible reports, "…God hath dealt to every man the measure of faith."

And it is the God kind of faith. He did not say, "a measure." He said "the measure." Everybody gets the same amount when they are filled with the Holy Ghost and are born again. It is not the problem that you don't have any faith, nor have you a smaller portion of faith, it is just that you have not developed the measure of faith God already gave you.

Now faith comes by hearing, and hearing by the Word of God. The literal translation of the Greek says, "Faith cometh by report, and that report comes from God." Hearing what God said will build faith inside you, because God is able to perform His every declaration in and through you. Now, what you hear by faith, you return to God by faith. What report I give you, you give it back to God. Faith-filled words are words that you come by through endurance of hearing. This is what Jesus said, For verily I say unto you, That whosoever shall say unto this mountain, Be thou removed, and be thou cast into the sea; and shall not doubt in his heart, but shall believe that those things which he saith shall come to pass; he shall have whatsoever he saith. Mark 11:23 (KJV) Here is the key to this scripture. Jesus said that if you believe the things you say, they shall come to past. You shall have whatsoever you say. Faith filled words are the words you truly believe.

Let's go back to that guy on the cliff, hanging on a branch. "Help, is there anyone up there?" "I'm here says the Lord." "Then you must help me." The Lord said, "Then let go of the branch." He replies, "Is anyone else up there?" You get your answer. Your prayer is answered, but you don't like the solution. The solution does not appease your fleshy concerns and fears. Even though it is God talking to you, you ask, "Is there anyone else up there." This is the epitome of, COSMETIC SUPERFICIAL FAITH (CSF). CSF is the plight of many Christians who cannot overcome their fear. This faith is cosmetic because it is only put on. It is superficial because it is not believed deep within. Any storm in your life can be tranquilized by faith-filled words. Any fear you have can be subdued by speaking with the authority that the Lord gives His followers.

The more faith we have in Christ, the more we'll be at peace, realizing the storms have no power over us. In fact, the power of our faith-filled words is one of the primary reasons we can have faith in the storm. It is in the storm when true believers are at their strongest. It is in the storm when we have our greatest opportunities. It is in the storm when miracles are most likely to occur. It is in the storm when the Holy Ghost is more apt increase our wisdom. It is in the storm when Jesus sleeps, waiting to see just how much faith we have.

Jesus is sleeping on a pilot's pillow wondering which one of them on deck will tell that storm to be quiet. Jesus is waiting on which disciple will display the faith that he has taught them and tell those waves to be still. Jesus is waiting of someone who truly believes in Him to tell that wind to stop blowing. You're waiting on Jesus, but Jesus is waiting on you. Too many Christians love to say "God is able." He sure is. But you are supposed to be able through Jesus Christ.

Power is authority. Jesus has given the authority to us to speak to all manner of storms. Fear is the enemy because God did not give us that kind of spirit. All fear must be overcome to effectuate God's living power. The disappointment Jesus expressed was that no one was willing to stand up to the storm. The Bible says that there were many little ships on the sea as well. We can imagine that thousands of people may have been out there on that rough water and not one had the courage to stand up to the storm.

Speaking to storms is the duty of believers. Calming trouble is our business as well. We are peacemakers. The true manifestation of God's spirit in us is verified by our willingness to take on the problems. We, as believers, can not sit idly by while the enemy destroys our homes, families, jobs and communities. There are some storms we must deal with.

Reflection: I am well aware that it will take a keen sense of faith to tackle some storms. However, that is our calling! God's living power must be utilized and trusted, even if we are afraid. The fear must be overcome and the faith must go forth. Trust God!

PowerPoints!

- **Stop trying to cling to your safety net.**
- **Real courage is the absence of fear.**
- **Trust God ...for real!**
- **It's either sink or swim, you might as well swim.**
- **Call on Him and believe in Him.**

CHAPTER TWELVE

POWER TO KNOW WE ARE NOT ALONE

In 2 Kings 6 (KJV), Elisha's servant got up one morning, he saw the invading army of King Ben-Hadad, the king of Syria. The servant cried out, "alas, my master! What shall we do?" But Elisha said to the servant, "Fear not: for they that be with us are more than they that be with them." Elisha wanted the young man to see beyond his fear; see beyond his anxiety; see beyond his weakness; see beyond his doubt; see beyond his present trouble. Elisha wanted this young man to see that with God possibility is more probability. Elisha wanted him to understand that when you are in God's favor you are never alone. Even though your enemy has encamped all around you must learn to focus and realize that they that be with us are more than they that be with them! Chuck Swindoll often says, "Faith alone saves, but the faith that saves is never alone".

The problem with many of us is that we become mesmerized with our problem, focused only on that which appears to be imminent. Elisha wanted God to give the young man spiritual eyes to focus on the awesomeness of God's potential. Believers never go into battle alone. The armies of the Lord constantly are doing battle on behalf of God's children.

Question: Are you aware of your angel support?

Angels often are involved in carrying out the judgment destruction orders of the Lord. They also fight off demonic forces that are often aimed directly at us. They marshal power and contend with satanic contentions.

When Lot was called by God to come out of Sodom, the Lord sent angels to deliver Lot and his wife and children. Angels later literally destroyed the city of Sodom in response to the command of God. Angels smote Herod because of his sin against God and the Bible says he was eaten of worms and died. In Psalms 35 (KJV), when David speaks of his enemies, he says, "Let the angel of the Lord chase them, let the angel of the Lord persecute them." Elisha says to the young man, "Fear not: for they that be with us are more that they that be with them." It should be obvious that angels are involved in the deliverance of God's people that have worked their way into His favor. There are angelic undertakings, under-girding and assistance. "Bless the LORD, ye his angels, that excel in strength, that do his commandments, hearkening unto the voice of his word." (Psalms 103:20, KJV) We are not alone. Therefore we fight with the confidence that our numbers are always superior and we consistently have the high ground.

Another Question: Are you afraid?

So many Christians are struggling, seeking a better definition of faith. Allow me to help; you've got to have guts. Faith can be characterized as guts (courage); the firm belief that God will never forsake you and no enemy can defeat you. You plus God are a majority. Too many believers are not truly believers. They are hope-ers. They hope God will not desert them. They hope that God will financially bless them. They hope that God will eventually heal them. Please do not misunderstand me. I am not anti-hope I'm pro-substance. Thomas Aquinas wrote, "Faith has to do with things that are not seen and hope with things that are not at hand." My hoping is based on my faith. My hoping is not sufficient in itself. Therefore, my faith goes to the substance of my beliefs. Augustine once proclaimed, "God's mercy … goes before the unwilling to make him willing; it follows the willing to make his will effectual." The child of God must learn to focus on victory and never focus on defeat! With God all things are possible and there are always more of us than of them. God's angels are involved in our battles. Although the Holy Spirit lives within all Christians, not all Christians are directed and empowered by Him. The Bible tells us there are three kinds of people: natural, spiritual and carnal, representing different responses to God (1 Corinthians 2:12 - 3:3). We are natural people, but we must operate in the spiritual. A carnal representation will limit our ability within our own capability. A spiritual ability goes beyond our natural limits.

The unfortunate dilemma is that we are well acquainted with our weaknesses therefore our faith only reaches to the extent of what we deem our capability. God deals in the realm of complete possibility. There is no measure by which His reach can be determined; this is what we must remember. It's not us alone. It is us with God's reach. One night a house caught fire and a young boy was forced to flee to the roof. The father stood on the ground below with outstretched arms, calling to his son, "Jump! I'll catch you." He knew the boy had to jump to save his life. All the boy could see, however, was flame, smoke, and blackness. As can be imagined, he was afraid to leave the roof. His father kept yelling: "Jump! I will catch you." But the boy protested, "Daddy, I can't see you." The father replied, "But I can see you and that's all that matters." What we can see is of little importance. What matters is what God can see. A leap of faith is just that, a leap!

The 21st century believer must become knowledgeable of the authority the Lord gives to each of us that truly believe. In a world of Bin Laden's, train bombings, drive-by shootings, school ground mass murders and anthrax; a child of God needs to understand his privilege on earth as a believer. The Word of God declares that the night is spent and the day is at hand. Let us therefore cast off the works of darkness (ignorance). And let us put on the armor of light (intelligence). Hosea said, "My people are destroyed for lack of knowledge. I will also reject thee, that thou shalt be no priest to me: seeing thou hast forgotten the law of thy God, I will also forget thy children." (Hosea 4:6, KJV) Ignorance is inexcusable under God. Civil law may offer some relief for ignorance of laws, but God's Word states clearly that God rejects those that reject knowledge.

Here's a thought: Praise is a weapon for spiritual warfare!

The enemy has his imps but we have angels. Angels wait for us to get active in spiritual warfare before they actually carry out the spiritual equivalent of what the believers pray for. God's effectual will for us is to have victory over the enemy. The evidence of our involvement that serves as the launching platform for God's angels is praise. When believers move into the plan of God for their lives and give evidence by engaging in spiritual warfare with their praise, angels are freed by God to do what they have always wanted to do, destroy, maintain and control the enemies of God. Angels of God will only begin to move on our behalf when the church begins to recognize its authority and learns to focus on the manifestation of God's power instead of focusing on the extent of our problems. Praise in the face of disaster is faith. The ability to praise God in spite of present problems is aromatic, even mesmeric to angels. They can't resist it! Forest Wood's book, THE ARROGANCE OF FAITH, gives evidence that faith sometimes appears arrogant, but in reality it is confidence. God delights in faithfulness, even if it sometimes appears arrogant.

The Bible teaches us that God is penchant to deliver his people based on their spiritual engagement and involvement. The religious do not qualify. The sanctimonious do not qualify. The self-righteous do not qualify. Good church folk do not qualify. But those that worship Him in spirit in truth, the true worshippers, qualify for this kind of deliverance. God will set ambushments against your enemies, but you need holy eyes that can focus on victory to see God's setup. The "guts factor" is your willingness to have courage, believe and trust God. This becomes faith in action. The move of action is the move of faith. Faith is having the guts to press ahead.

When Balaam disobeyed the Lord and God was angry with him, God sent an angel to carry out His vengeance. Balaam's ass saw the angel but Balaam did not (**Numbers 22:28 KJV**). When the Lord finally opened the eyes of Balaam, he was the angel and fell on his face. God sets ambushments with His angels. When Elisha is at Dothan and his servant saw Ben-Hadad's army all around them, Elisha prayed to God that this young man would be able to focus on their victory instead of focusing on the size of Ben-Hadad's army. There were more angels with Elisha than Assyrians in Ben-Hadad's army. Again remember what David said in Psalm 35, "Let the angel of the Lord chase them." Now we need to examine this particular fact. In the Holy Bible, God's ambushments usually coincide exactly with the time that the children of Israel begin to sing and praise the Lord. Again praise in the face of adversity is faith. Prayer coupled with praise is the action of faith that triggers God's supernatural forces on our behalf.

Consider more evidence, in Acts 12:5 (KJV); Herod killed James, the brother of John with a sword. Then he put Peter in prison, "but prayer was made without ceasing of the church unto God for Peter." The church immediately began to intercede for Peter. What happened? The angel of the Lord came to Peter in the prison, delivered him, and set him free from the jail. This indicates the connection between the prayer of God's children and the activity of angels.

Question: Do you truly know the Lord?

Power to live can only come by the grace of God. The grace of God can only come by knowledge of God. In other words a person must first know God to be qualified for His grace. Grace is not available to those who do not know the Lord Jesus Christ in the pardon of their sins. Regardless of what you hear, and where you may hear it, grace is the unmerited favor bestowed upon a believer of Jesus Christ. It is our knowledge of Him that enables us through His grace. Knowing God is a matter of personal dealing. Knowing God is more than just knowing about Him; it is a matter of having a relationship with him as He opens up to you. J. L. Packer once wrote, "Knowing about Him is a necessary precondition of trusting in Him." To get to know another person, you have to commit yourself to his company and interests, and be ready to identify yourself with his concerns. Without this, you cannot build a meaningful relationship.

Now in the case of human beings, knowing them is complicated by the fact that, unlike God, people keep secrets and lie. God, however, is not a man that will tell you a lie. People don't always show you what is in their heart. But God opened His heart and showed us His love for us through Jesus Christ. "But God, who is rich in mercy, for his great love wherewith he loved us, Even when we were dead in sins, hath quickened us together with Christ, (by grace ye are saved;) And hath raised us up together, and made us sit together in heavenly places in Christ Jesus." Ephesians 2:4-6 (KJV)

Normally our difficulty becomes even greater when we think about our inability to please God; our ability to change sinful habits for good ones. What we find is that without God's intervention, we can do nothing. Our knowledge of God gives us companionship with Him. It is all in the knowing. We will never be alone as long as our understanding intensifies our relationship with Him. Augustine was once accosted by a heathen who showed him his idol and said, "Here is my god; where is thine?" Augustine replied, "I cannot show you my God; not because there is no God to show but because you have no eyes to see Him." We must have eyes to see Him, His works and His presence. We are never alone!

Reflection: I am well aware that my bluntness may make some uncomfortable. However, I truly believe that you cannot gently wake some people. There are those you must shake and those that need a strong voice. This book is designed to be a wake-up call.

PowerPoints!

- **My problems are not bigger than my God.**
- **I must have guts, faith-based guts!**
- **My hoping is not sufficient in itself, I must believe.**
- **I must operate in the realm of complete possibility.**
- **My faith must be strong, even if it appears arrogant.**
- **My true power is in my spirit, not my might.**
- **My spiritual ability goes beyond my limitations.**

CHAPTER THIRTEEN

THE POWER OF LEARNING HOW TO WAIT

G. Campbell Morgan said, "Waiting for God is not laziness. Waiting for God is not going to sleep. Waiting for God is not the abandonment of effort. Waiting for God means, first, activity under command; second, readiness for any new command that may come; third, the ability to do nothing until the command is given." Let's consider two Old Testament scriptures, Habakkuk 2:3 (KJV) and Ecclesiastes 3:1 (KJV), Habakkuk writes, "For the vision is yet for an appointed time, but at the end it shall speak, and not lie: though it tarry, wait for it; because it will surely come, it will not tarry." The writer of Ecclesiastes adds, "To every thing there is a season, and a time to every purpose under the heaven." To borrow from Bishop T. D. Jakes, I may be delayed but not denied. The word of God says that everyone that is born of a woman will have days that are filled with trouble. This is not a comforting thought because according to the syntax this trouble is not escapable. We all are born of women; even the women. Psalms 27:14 (KJV) states, "Wait on the LORD: be of good courage, and he shall strengthen thine heart: wait, I say, on the LORD." A better understanding of this concept of waiting is found in the book of Isaiah. While we all know the words of this passage my memory, we may not know the words that set up the passage. To get a clear understanding of what God is saying let's consider the verses of Isaiah 40:28 – 31 (KJV), "Hast thou not known? hast thou not heard, that the everlasting God, the LORD, the Creator of the ends of the earth, fainteth not, neither is weary? there is no searching of his understanding. He giveth power to the faint;

and to them that have no might he increaseth strength. Even the youths shall faint and be weary, and the young men shall utterly fall: But they that wait upon the LORD shall renew their strength; they shall mount up with wings as eagles; they shall run, and not be weary; and they shall walk, and not faint."

Just a note: Grandmamma would say, "Trouble does not last always."

We are often like Lucy in the "Peanuts" comic strip. Lucy was complaining about her lousy life. Charley Brown is trying to cheer her up. "Into each life some rain must fall," he said. That didn't seem to help at all. Then he thought of another saying: "Just remember, life has its mountains and its valleys, its ups and downs." To which Lucy replied, "All I want is ups and ups and ups!" Like Lucy, so many of us just want the "ups." But every child of God will have seasons of trouble, struggle and testing. Trouble, just like the love of the Lord, is promised to you. The Apostle Paul calls these troubles, "light afflictions." "For our light affliction, which is but for a moment, worketh for us a far more exceeding and eternal weight of glory." (2 Corinthians 4:17, KJV) Our true struggle is in the waiting, it is not the trouble itself, but it is the expectation of our coming "season."

Christmas Day is the result of many generations of Hebrews waiting for the coming of the Messiah. Through great adversity they waited for a Bethlehem morning. They waited so long that we the day finally came and Christ was born into the world, some of them refused to believe it. A person can become so accustomed to trouble that struggle becomes normal and success becomes abnormal. The Jews had waited so long that they became comfortable with their suffering and oppression. Their failure to recognize their Savior was the product of their impatience.

God is a God of order. Everything happens by divine decree. We cannot force it, nor can we hurry it up. Even our prayers won't get a heavenly rush job. We just have to wait. Do not be confused with the thesis of previous chapters that there are hills for us to climb and rivers for us to cross. There is always something we can do, while we wait on divine intervention. We exercise our gifts and anointing in the reality that there will always be things we'll just have to wait for.

Paul says that trouble crowns us with a higher glory. Therefore it is that high state of glory that must accompany us coming into our season. If we revisit Ecclesiastes 3 we will see a God of order, "To every thing there is a season, and a time to every purpose under the heaven: A time to be born, and a time to die; a time to plant, and a time to pluck up that which is planted; A time to kill, and a time to heal; a time to break down, and a time to build up; A time to weep, and a time to laugh; a time to mourn, and a time to dance; A time to cast away stones, and a time to gather stones together; a time to embrace, and a time to refrain from embracing; A time to get, and a time to lose; a time to keep, and a time to cast away; A time to rend, and a time to sew; a time to keep silence, and a time to speak; A time to love, and a time to hate; a time of war, and a time of peace." (Ecclesiastes 3: 1 – 8, KJV) And in verse eleven God's purpose for this order is clarified, "He hath made every thing beautiful in his time: also he hath set the world in their heart, so that no man can find out the work that God maketh from the beginning to the end." (Ecclesiastes 3:11, KJV)

Here's a thought: Hurry up and wait!

It is the charge of every true worshipper to trust God to the point that they can say in the face of adversity, "This too shall pass." God has predetermined a certain time to bring to pass His promise in our lives. The appointment has already been made. We are not denied, just delayed. Our trust in God enables us to declare, "My time is coming." We should have an inner awareness that understands even though times may be difficult now, my season is coming. Even though the road seems tough, my season is coming. Even though every enemy seems ready to destroy me, my season is coming. Even though the bills are mounting up, my season is coming. God has a present time of deliverance. Our comfort is in the knowing that because of our confession of Jesus as Lord and Savior, we have an appointment on the book. Our time is coming. It is not always accomplished by our human might and intelligence, but through His Spirit. "Then he answered and spake unto me, saying, This is the word of the LORD unto Zerubbabel, saying, Not by might, nor by power, but by my spirit, saith the LORD of hosts." (Zechariah 4:6, KJV) Abraham and

Sarah waited and God gave them Issac. Zacharias and Elizabeth waited and God gave them John the Baptist.

God unwrapped the blanket of failure from around Adam and Eve and set in motion an appointed time for the Messiah to come into the world. Abraham waited, Jacob waited, Isaac waited, David waited, Solomon waited, Isaiah waited, Elijah waited, Ezekiel waited, Daniel waited, Shadrach, Meshach and Abednego waited, Nehemiah waited, Amos, Obadiah, Nahum, Joel, Micah and all the other prophets waited. But on one winter morning shepherds waited while tending their flocks. And the announcement came, the wait is over, He is born in Bethlehem.

God's purpose for you can only be aborted when you refuse to trust Him and wait. Satan is attempting to assassinate the will of God in your life. Satan wants to destroy God's purpose for you. It is during the course of "the wait," that the enemy attacks you with notions of personal failure and the lack of God's love. More than anyone else, David understood the need for waiting, "I waited patiently for the LORD; and he inclined unto me, and heard my cry. He brought me up also out of an horrible pit, out of the miry clay, and set my feet upon a rock, and established my goings. And he hath put a new song in my mouth, even praise unto our God: many shall see it, and fear, and shall trust in the LORD." (Psalms 40: 1 – 3, KJV)

I'm often disturbed when I make a phone call to a business or office and the receptionist immediately upon answering says, "Would you please hold on?" Without a hello or greeting of any type the hold button is pushed. The real test of faith is in facing the silence of being put on hold. Just because you are on hold does not mean God will not answer. It is not that you are placed in a purgatory, caught betwixt and between, but rather placed on a runway waiting to take off. Like the pilot, we too must wait on the control tower to give us the command to go. We must understand that God's timing is not like our timing. God's delivery system works on a heavenly agenda, not an earthly plain. The Jewish nation waited for the coming of the Messiah. Through great travail, persecution, and oppression they waited. God never forgot them, and God will never forget you. You have an appointed time to harvest. You have a season coming. You're on the runway just waiting to take off!

Reflection: Patience has always been my weak point. However I have learned that God's agenda does include me, therefore, I'm learning to wait. While I'm waiting I'm practicing everything else I have learned concerning power-connected living. I'm waiting, but I'm working, believing and trusting!

PowerPoints!

- Patience is a virtue. With God it's a directive!
- Hurry up and learn how to wait!
- Repeat daily, "My season is coming."
- God's timing is not our timing!
- Deliverance only comes when its time.

CHAPTER FOURTEEN

POWER TO KNOW DROUGHTS WILL END AND THE RAINS WILL COME

There comes a time when we all will experience a drought of some type. It may be the drought of health when it seems like there is no end in sight to your physical problems. It may be the drought of finances when it seems like the bills are coming in faster than the money to pay them. It may be the drought of your occupation because the stress of your job doesn't seem to be justified by your salary. There may be a drought in your marriage or relationships because personal strain and tension. But of all the droughts I can think of, probably the worst is a spiritual drought. We have all had them. You pray but you feel like the prayers are answered. You read your Bible but it does not seem to help. Elijah gives us some good news. Whatever your drought, the drought is ending and the rains are coming. And that is what we should desire for each one of our lives: that the drought will end and the rains will come. Israel has been without rain for nearly 3 years. "And it came to pass after many days, that the word of the LORD came to Elijah in the third year, saying, Go, shew thyself unto Ahab; and I will send rain upon the earth. And Elijah went to shew himself unto Ahab. And there was a sore famine in Samaria." (1 Kings 18: 1, 2, KJV) Let's continue with the biblical account, "And Elijah said unto Ahab, Get thee up, eat and drink; for there is a sound of abundance of rain. So Ahab went up to eat and to drink. And Elijah went up to the top of Carmel; and he cast himself down upon the earth, and put his face between his knees, And said to his servant, Go up now, look toward the sea. And he went up, and looked, and said, there is nothing. And he said, Go again seven times. And it came to pass at the seventh time, that he said, Behold, there ariseth a little cloud out of the sea, like a man's hand. And he said, Go up, say unto Ahab, Prepare thy chariot, and get thee down, that the rain stop thee not. And it came to pass in the mean while, that the heaven was black with clouds and wind, and there was a great rain. And Ahab rode, and went to Jezreel." (1 Kings 18: 41 – 45. KJV)

Here's a thought: Sometimes trouble is God attempting to get our attention!

God sent Elijah to King Ahab to challenge the beliefs of the people. In this eighteenth chapter we find, the sad state of Israel at this time. Jezebel cut off the prophets of the Lord and killed them. Jezebel was an idolater, she was a persecutor, and she turned Ahab in to one. Even in those bad times, when the calves were worshipped and the temple at Jerusalem deserted, there were still some good people that feared God and served him, and some good prophets that instructed them in the knowledge of him and assisted them in their worship. God had punished Israel with a drought. Sometimes its punishment and sometimes God just wants to get our attention. Droughts always come because of disobedience. They don't always come because of sinful disobedience, but because God wants to know whom you are serving. "And Elijah came unto all the people, and said, how long halt ye between two opinions? If the LORD be God, follow him: but if Baal, then follow him. And the people answered him not a word." (1 Kings 18:21, KJV)

We must remember, disobedience comes many different ways:
1. Directly
2. Indirectly
3. Permissively
4. Ignorantly
5. Apathetically

Any of the above can cause a drought. In the time of Ahab and Jezebel, it was not just their sinful idolatry; it was the people's apathy that caused the drought. With apathy they watched Jezebel kill the prophets of God, now God must send a prophet that will kill their prophets. You know the story; Elijah challenged the prophets of Baal. "Then said Elijah unto the people, I, even I only, remain a prophet of the LORD; but Baal's prophets are four hundred and fifty men. Let them therefore give us two bullocks; and let them choose one bullock for themselves, and cut it in pieces, and lay it on wood, and put no fire under: and I will dress the other bullock, and lay it on wood, and put no fire under: And call ye on the name of your gods, and I will call on the name of the LORD: and the God that answereth by fire, let him be God." (1 Kings 18: 22 – 24, KJV) Elijah proposed to bring the matter to a trial. Baal had all the outward advantages, but the event encourages all God's witnesses and advocates never to fear the face of man. Here's what's going to happen, the God that answers by fire, let him be God. In the Old Testament times man's atonement was to be made by sacrifice, before the judgment could be removed in mercy. Since the death and resurrection of Christ mercy has been extended because of Jesus and the ultimate sacrifice and atonement has been made. So according to Elijah, the God that has power to pardon sin, and to signify it by consuming the sin-offering, must be the God that can end the drought. "And they (the prophets of Baal) cried aloud, and cut themselves after their manner with knives and lancets, till the blood gushed out upon them. And it came to pass, when midday was past, and they prophesied until the time of the offering of the evening sacrifice, that there was neither voice, nor any to answer, nor any that regarded." (1 Kings 18: 28, 29, KJV)

My late brother-in-law, Elder James Watkins used to say, "There is a difference between prophesying and prophet-lying." Let me now read the historical account in 1 Kings 18 verses 30 – 40 (KJV), "And Elijah said unto all the people, Come near unto me. And all the people came near unto him. And he repaired the altar of the LORD that was broken down. And Elijah took twelve stones, according to the number of the tribes of the sons of Jacob, unto whom the word of the LORD came, saying, Israel shall be thy name: And with the stones he built an altar in the name of the LORD: and he made a trench about the altar, as great as would contain two measures of seed. And he put the wood in order, and cut the bullock in pieces, and laid him on the wood, and said, Fill four barrels with water, and pour it on the burnt sacrifice, and on the wood. And he said, Do it the second time. And they did it the second time. And he said, Do it the third time. And they did it the third time. And the water ran round about the altar; and he filled the trench also with water. And it came to pass at the time of the offering of the evening sacrifice, that Elijah the prophet came near, and said, LORD God of Abraham, Isaac, and of Israel, let it be known this day that thou art God in Israel, and that I am thy servant, and that I have done all these things at thy word. Hear me, O LORD, hear me, that this people may know that thou art the LORD God, and that thou hast turned their heart back again. Then the fire of the LORD fell, and consumed the burnt sacrifice, and the wood, and the stones, and the dust, and licked up the water that was in the trench. And when all the people saw it, they fell on their faces: and they said, The LORD, he is the God; the LORD, he is the God. And Elijah said unto them, Take the prophets of Baal; let not one of them escape. And they took them: and Elijah brought them down to the brook Kishon, and slew them there."

Just a thought: Your arms are too short to box with God!

Four hundred fifty prophets are put to death and the people now worship Jehovah. God is now prepared to end the drought. Isn't it interesting that sometimes God wants something killed before he will bless you? Sometimes God wants you to make a decision to kill something within you that is unpleasing to Him. Droughts can be turned around with a willingness to confront those issues that leave God wanting.

"And Elijah said to Ahab, Go, eat and drink, for there is the sound of a heavy rain.

So Ahab went off to eat and drink, but Elijah climbed to the top of Carmel, bent down to the ground and put his face between his knees." (1 Kings 18: 41, 42 NIV)

"And said to his servant, Go up now, look toward the sea. And he went up, and looked, and said, There is nothing. And he said, Go again seven times. And it came to pass at the seventh time, that he said, Behold, there ariseth a little cloud out of the sea, like a man's hand. And he said, Go up, say unto Ahab, Prepare thy chariot, and get thee down, that the rain stop thee not. And it came to pass in the mean while, that the heaven was black with clouds and wind, and there was a great rain." (1 Kings 18: 43 – 45 NIV)

Seven times Elijah sent his servant to look toward the sea to see any sign that the rains are coming. The Bible doesn't tell us what Elijah is doing while he sends his servant is off looking but I can tell you what he is doing: he is praying for the rains to come. He is no less persistent the seventh time than he was the first time. He was persistence despite the fact there was no evidence that the rain was coming. How many of you would have quit after the first time, the second time, the third time? Surely we would have quit by the fifth time. I've got to go to God again and again, believing that my rain is coming!

Do you know: Big things come in little packages!

Then some of us can't see our victory in little blessings. There ariseth a "little cloud." Sometimes God prepares us for the ultimate victory with a little victory. If I am going to come out of my drought, I must have faith that the smallest cloud can produce the mightiest storm. The Bible is full of cases where something small became big in the hands of God. The little boy's lunch in the hands of God fed 5,000; the small stone in the hands of David killed a giant; the small town of Bethlehem became the birthplace of the Savior. Sometimes we don't get our rain because we haven't given up our small things into the hands of a big God. If I am having financial problems I am going to put whatever small amount of money I have into the hands of God. If I only have a little bit of time, I am going to put that into the hands of a big God. If I only have a little bit of health I am going to put that into the hands of a big God. It's going to rain. Droughts don't last forever. God will take your driest days and turn them in to bountiful showers.

I'm reminded of a story told by a pastor in New York City. When he and his family arrived in New York to take on his new pastorate, he had difficulty finding the church. He pulled over to the curb and asked a man that appeared to be a street person, "Excuse me, but do you know where the First Calvary church is located?" The man replied, "Yes sir, just turn your car around and go to the end of this street and you'll see the church on the corner. The pastor, realizing that he was on a one-way street replied,

"I can't turn around here, can you give me other directions?" The man quipped quickly, "I told you, just turn around and go straight up this street and you'll see the church." The pastor quickly realized that the only way the man knew was the way he would walk to the church. Sometimes we just need to turn around.

Reflection: The Bible is replete with droughts and what usually causes them. It is up to the believer to realize that our droughts come the same way. God will do whatever He has to do to gain our attention. Learn to act correctively!

PowerPoints!

- **Pray the victory, don't pray the problem.**
- **Listen as God speaks to you.**
- **Confront the issues that separate you from God.**
- **Disobedience may come in the form of apathy.**
- **Don't fight God, you'll lose!**
- **Always be willing to turn around.**

EPILOGUE

The Greek word translated physical body means slave. The physical body should be a slave to the human spirit. Sin caused the human spirit to lose control over the body. Adam became a spiritually dead man the moment he sinned. He became body-ruled, and not spirit-ruled. Charles Capps in his book, RELEASING THE ABILITY OF GOD THROUGH PRAYER says, "The spirit man was dethroned that very hour; the human spirit lost its authority and ability to rule the body. Sin took control of the flesh. The body rose up and began to rule over the spirit." Therefore we can understand why the Apostle Paul said in Romans 8:6 (KJV), "For to be carnally minded is death; but to be spiritually minded is life and peace." Then the mouth is the reflection of the inner spirit. What comes out the mouth reflects what's inside the spirit of man. Faith filled words release God, and unscriptural talk cancels prayer.

POWER TO LIVE is the continual message I teach and preach. A person's praying and saying must compliment each other. God's Word says that man shall have whatsoever he saith, if he believes and doubts not in his heart. The earth was spawned from the spirit world. It was created to be the likeness of the spiritual world, which spawned it. Man was created by God to be in the likeness of God: to have dominion, to control, and to rule. Your spirit should control your body, and your mouth should bear the reflection of the spirit of God that is in you. God's kingdom ruleth over all, and He set up His kingdom inside us. The Holy Ghost is God in us. It is the indwelling of God's Spirit that must have control over our bodies, but especially our mouths. James declares that controlling the mouth is the method by which we can control the body, "Behold, we put bits in the horses' mouths, that they may obey us; and we turn about their whole body." (James 3:3, KJV)

To be carnally minded is to be out of control and body-ruled; it produces spiritual death. To be spiritually minded is to be spirit-ruled, and it will produce life and peace, because God designed you that way. Romans 8:2 (KJV) states, "For the law of the Spirit of life in Christ Jesus hath made me free from the law of sin and death." God's law that produces spirit life in Christ made your spirit free from the spiritual death caused by sin.

The Law was given to people who were body-ruled. Body-ruled people cannot obey the laws of God because God wants one thing and their bodies want another. The flesh is weak; it is not subject to God's laws. All the people from Adam to Jesus were body-ruled; their spirits were slaves to their bodies. It was a satanic chain that enslaved all mankind. Then Jesus came to the earth, in the likeness of sinful flesh. He looked like other men, but God was His Father and He was spirit-ruled. Jesus broke the satanic chain of spirit slavery and condemned sin that had enthroned itself in the earth. Jesus brought down the satanic stronghold and made it possible for men to walk in the spirit. Look at Romans 8:10 (KJV), "And if Christ be in you, the body is dead because of sin but the Spirit is life because of righteousness." When Christ comes into your spirit, the body dies; it is dethroned. The Spirit of God now rules over you and your mouth reflects the spirit within. The body is dead, but the spirit is life because of righteousness. The spirit man received the ability to rule the body once again.

Now the spirit person grows on the Word of God. God's Word is filled with faith and that feeds the spirit person. John wrote in 6:63 (KJV), "It is the spirit that quickeneth; the flesh profiteth nothing: the words that I speak unto you, they are spirit, and they are life." It takes time to train the spirit, but god's Words are spirit life. The process of training the spirit life is the process of perfecting or power building.

Say only the things that you believe and they will come to pass. Quit talking foolishness, sickness and disease (example: "I'm catching a cold). The mouth is the representative of the spirit within. Learn to control what you say, and never speak anything that you don't want to come to pass. God's Word says that man shall have whatsoever he saith, if he believes and doubts not in his heart. Whatsoever things ye desire when ye pray, believe ye receive them. What is the voice of God's Word? The Bible is His written word, but you must give it voice.

All heaven will stand behind what you say. Remember prayer is not telling God your problem and prayer is not you trying to change God's mind. Prayer is declaration of belief and faith. Your need does not move God to action in your life; it is your faith that moves God. Praying the same prayer over and over does not cause God to move; your faith action does. Mark 11:24 (KJV) says, "What things soever ye desire, when ye pray, believe that ye receive them, and ye shall have them." The spirit-controlled person releases this faith principle and God responds to the faith of the believer. Religious praying will not serve your spiritual interest. This is praying just because it seems right to pray. Prayer must be a companion of faith-walking, which only comes from a spirit-controlled person, and it is reflected by the words of the person from the spirit within.

POWER TO LIVE comes from God's presence within. Stop accepting the mundane. Stop approving the mediocre. Stop indulging the insignificant. Stand up now and speak faith-filled words. Rise in the awesomeness and power of God's spirit.

ABOUT THE AUTHOR

Active and alert to the needs of the people, Dr. Bill Adkins has stood before mayors, governors, presidents and international dignitaries on behalf of causes and concerns. He is recognized around the world as a humanitarian and scholar. This former broadcast journalist is regarded as a broadcast icon in Memphis where he was a TV News Anchor and radio Talk Show Host. He is a charismatic leader and provocative thinker, responsible for numerous initiatives in Memphis and around the world. He is a much sought after speaker and lecturer.

This visionary leader started Greater Imani Church and Christian Center in Memphis, Tennessee on November 1, 1989 with 29 dedicated friends and family members. Since that time, Greater Imani has enjoyed phenomenal growth, making it one of the largest congregations in Memphis.

His missions and ministries continue to bless people around the world. Dr. Adkins has led numerous missionary journeys to Africa and the Caribbean, establishing health clinics in Koalack Senegal, Banjul, Gambia and Kumasi, Ghana. A global humanitarian, he has actively supported numerous economic development efforts on the African continent. He is credited with delivering over five million dollars in medicines, medical supplies and equipment to West Africa. He received the distinction of being one of the few Americans enstooled as an Ashanti Chief in Ghana. He has widely traveled the world, preaching and teaching on five of the six habitable continents.

He has been featured on DAN RATHER REPORTS, and has been interviewed by the BBC, NBC, Australia's Today Program and USA Today Newspaper. His sermons have been featured in THE AFRICAN

AMERICAN PULPIT magazine, HOPE AND HEALING, and his sermon A DREAM FULFILLED is now posted in the Library of Congress.

Our author holds degrees in History, Theology and Divinity and is the recipient of an honorary doctorate. He is a graduate of the Harvard Divinity College Leadership Institute (2007) and was voted by readers of the Memphis Commercial Appeal Newspaper as Memphis' Most Passionate Preacher (2008). He has counseled and advised two presidents and continues to be instrumental in the causes and concerns of our citizens, serving on numerous boards and committees, including St. Jude Children's Research Hospital. He has served as national chaplain of his fraternity, Kappa Alpha Psi.

His TV program, also titled, POWER TO LIVE is seen weekly; nationally and internationally, on the WORD NETWORK, reaching over 93 million homes in the United States and the Caribbean, along with over 200 countries in Europe, Africa, Asia and Australia.

He is the author of numerous books including: FROM AFRICA TO BETHLEHEM, LIVING IN THE SPIRIT and THANK YOU FOR TALKING ABOUT ME, sold in bookstore nationwide.

He is married to the lovely Linda Kerr Adkins and they have four children, Taihia L. Adkins, Dr. Ronne' A Adkins, Christopher G. Adkins and William A. Adkins III.

Printed in the United States
By Bookmasters